VANISHED

IN THE WOODS:

THE MISSING
THE DROWNED
AND THE DEAD

Steph Young

Table of Contents

Introduction 4

Chapter One - The Missing Park Ranger 5

Chapter Two - The Vanished Boy 13

Chapter Three - Missing in the Smoky Mountains 18

Chapter Four - Missing Stacy Arias 30

Chapter Five - Secret Bases & The Missing 47

Chapter Six - The Missing Hunter 97

Chapter Seven - In the Sky & Underground 115

Chapter Eight - Dark-Eyed Abductors 140

Chapter Nine - Fallen Angels, the Dragon & The
    Missing 171

Chapter Ten - Missing in the Wild Highlands 203

Chapter Eleven - 'America's most bizarre unsolved
    mystery.' 210

Chapter Twelve - Two vanished in the woods 231

Chapter Thirteen - The Returned Children 246

Introduction

People are going missing in the wilderness.

Something in the woods is taking people. Something unknown that we cannot define; something that others have had the misfortune to encounter.

People are snatched soundlessly, never to be seen again. Or they are returned; dead.

Strange and highly unusual predators are in the woods. Highly intelligent. Very successful. And able to overpower someone in an instant.

Rumours of secret underground bases, snatch and grab teams, deadly experimentation, aliens and monsters of the unknown....

This is a puzzle. A deadly one. People are going missing in the woods. Here follow some very troubling and disturbing true accounts....

Chapter One

The Missing Park Ranger

On the official website for Pastimes Cabins RV Park & Campground, in The Great Okefenokee Swamp in Southeast Georgia, there is a section on the lore of the area; 'Documented paranormal stories of the unexplained and the unusual along with some pretty weird stuff that has happened in and around the Okefenokee Swamp,' they say. This includes 'UFO sightings, Alien abductions, Hauntings, Big Foot, Skunk Ape and Pig Man!'

One account is; 'UFO sighted on east side of swamp, May 1998. Sighting observed over several mile area. The editor of the local newspaper gave a description as 'a large shiny black object' which hovered for some time, then broke into smaller objects and flew away in different directions. No plausible explanation has ever been given for this sighting.'

It was the next item however which really took my attention; 'ALIEN ABDUCTION,' they write. 'In early 1996, a former Everglades National Park Ranger, on vacation from upstate New York, visited Okefenokee's West side for bird watching. He put his canoe in at Stephen Foster Park, and paddled over to Billy's Island. He did not return. His canoe was found that evening on Billy's Island.

Over the next few weeks, local, State and Federal officials started a search for the man, which escalated to an extremely extensive search.' 'Exhaustive searches of the Island were conducted, hand to hand searches combing the entire Island, turned up nothing. Heat-seeking infrared helicopters were brought in, sensitive enough to identify small animals; this man weighed over 300lbs. They turned up nothing. Bloodhounds were brought in; the hounds could not pick up a scent beyond a small loop. Cadaver dogs were brought in; they turned up nothing.'

'All hope was given up, until 40-plus days after his disappearance, a bedraggled man was seen by a boater leaning against a tree near the water's edge. A day after this sighting, a dazed man identified himself as the missing man to passing canoeists. He was brought to the hospital in a confused and disoriented state.'

'He was not very informative as to what had happened to him. The man insisted he'd been wandering aimlessly on the Island the whole time. The Island is a small well-used island. Federal, State and local officials involved in the searches do not buy his story,' wrote the Newspaper. 'He has never publicly stated he was abducted. Speculation around the swamp is, he was taken from the island without his knowledge, then returned sometime after the search had been scaled down, with his memory seemingly erased. A classic UFO abduction,' they say.

Was it? It's certainly a baffling tale and in fact by checking archives of Newspapers from back then, it appears that this disappearance did indeed happen. The man who went missing was called Mike Goodell and he was a former Ranger at Everglades National Park. He was 33 year's old at the time and working as a corrections officer. It happened on February 4th, 1996.

The Florida Times Union reported, 'He was off on a three-mile trip to Billy's Island, where he planned to spend the day exploring the ruins of an old logging community, park officials said. Goodell hasn't been seen since. Nearly a month later, the mystery of what happened to the Mount Morris, N.Y., corrections officer baffles family members, park rangers and the dozens of Georgia and Florida law officers who have searched for him.'

'Four to five campers a year get lost and have to be rescued at the refuge. But park rangers say they can't remember anyone who went in and didn't come out without being found.' "He was an excellent camper and trail man who knew enough to stay put if he got lost," William Goodell, his father said. "It was like a UFO sucked him up."

'His abandoned canoe was found on Billy's Island,

sparking a search that eventually involved more than 80 rescue workers, bloodhounds, cadaver dogs, and helicopters with sophisticated tracking devices.' A.P. News wrote, 'Former Everglades National Park Ranger Goodell disappeared Feb. 4 after paddling his canoe to Billy's Island, a desolate area in the swamp. Despite an intensive search of the eight-square-mile island, Goodell never was spotted until volunteers found him Friday on a trail near the spot where they had discovered his canoe early in the rescue operation. Searchers had given up looking for Goodell on the small island when the group stumbled across him.'

'Goodell was found 41 days later, on March 15, lying on a dock, semi-conscious, near the location where rangers found his canoe when he first disappeared - stunning those involved in the search. Many had given up on finding Goodell dead or alive. When found, Goodell was incoherent and required two days hospitalization before he was able to tell authorities what had happened. Goodell complained of having pain all over his body. Doctors said he was recovering quickly from dehydration, cuts, and insect bites.' 'He had tried to walk north to find his canoe on the four-by-two-mile island, but apparently became "confused" and continually walked in circles instead, he said.'

'During the search, Goodell's sister Catherine speculated he somehow might have been taken off the island and then returned, but he told officials he had been there the whole time.' Goodell says he lost more than 50 pounds during his ordeal, surviving on bugs, leaves, berries and swamp water. ``I just hung out. I just kept walking around."

'Goodell, 33, wandered endlessly through the thick foliage covering Billy's Island, an eight-square-mile piece of land in the famed southern swamp. Search parties using sophisticated equipment couldn't track him down.'

'Lost Feb. 4th, he was found Friday by park volunteers after he finally relocated his lost canoe. "They said, `Are you the guy that's missing? ' And I said, `Yeah!'" said the former ranger.' 'A camper since he was a teenager, and once a ranger at Everglades National Park, he concedes he may have walked in circles until he got lucky and found the canoe.'

'The disappearance baffled many of Goodell's family members and friends because of his experience as a former National Park Ranger and his extensive camping experience. A search involved more than 80 rescue workers, hounds, cadaver dogs and helicopters. After he returned to New York, many involved in the search cast doubt about Goodell's whereabouts during the search. They said it was impossible for the 5-foot-5, 275-pound man to avoid detection if he was on the Island, which is 2 miles wide and 4 miles long.'

Was he simply just lost on the tiny island and walking round and round in circles, as he thinks, or, did something really take him off the Island? – 'Exhaustive searches of the Island were conducted, hand to hand searches combing the entire Island turned up nothing. Heat seeking infrared helicopters were brought in, sensitive enough to identify small animals - this man weighed over 300lbs. They turned up nothing. Cadaver dogs were brought in, they turned up nothing.

Bloodhounds were brought in. The hounds could not pick up a scent beyond a small loop...'

Why couldn't they find him? Had he somehow been taken from the island during the time he was missing? If so, what had taken him... and what had really happened to him...? How could he have been walking around in circles on the tiny island, for 40 days and nights, and never been seen....?

Chapter Two

The Vanished Boy

When Breiton Scott Ackerman, aged 4, disappeared from a small creek, nothing was ever found; no body, no clothing and no scent, despite search dogs and five hundred people looking for him.

8 years later, his father tells KSTV; "I don't understand it, I don't like it, but you can't change it. It's over in an instant. You wish you could go back and say we shouldn't have gone down there that day, or I should have had him tied to my belt or something like that – but you can't do that," said his grieving father. "Water was the only thing that makes sense," he said, "And that still doesn't make sense."

Breiton had been fishing with his father and other relatives in a small creek when he disappeared. One minute he was there, standing next to the others, and the next minute he was simply gone.

He was with his father, two more adults and five other children that fateful day on May 22nd 2005 at Willow Creek, southeast of Alton, Iowa. He disappeared in the afternoon. His father said, "Everybody's just catching them (fish) and throwing them in the bucket, and I think I had looked across; I asked one of the kids, "Where'd Breiton go?" - It was just that quick. He was just standing by the bucket dumping fish in and boom... that was it...."

'Seven years later, police are still trying to unravel the mystery of what happened to Breiton. The boy simply vanished without a trace,' said the Sioux City Journal. 'Every May 22, his father visits the spot where his son disappeared, desperate for an answer. Normally a shallow creek, when his little boy vanished, the creek, which runs through a cornfield, was swollen with rain. It was presumed he drowned — yet despite the huge search in the creek for his body, it was not found.'

In the hours that followed his disappearance, a desperate and frantic search of Willow Creek began. Gates were placed downstream as a precaution. Divers, search dogs and many volunteers scoured the creek, but they found no sign of him. Searchers followed the creek for 17 miles to the Floyd River in Le Mars Iowa, then they searched the river down to Missouri River. Many believed he had to have fallen off the bridge into the creek and drowned, but extensive searches by divers failed to find his body, and dogs, search crews, volunteers and helicopters overhead turned up no clues. The small concrete bridge on which the little boy had been standing was pulled up by searchers. The creek bed was dug up with industrial lifting equipment. "They dug down and back in the bank to make sure he didn't fall in a hole or was covered up. All the culverts that had to come out were searched with people and dogs, just looking for any clothing, any stitching," said his Father. "He had bare feet. He's like me – tender feet. I can't stand to walk on cement hardly with bare feet," he told reporters, "So he wouldn't have just run up the hill. Nobody came down that road to where we were," he says, ruling out any possibility of a abduction by a stranger.

Sioux County Sheriff Dan Altena said tidal experts estimated, that if the little boy had been in the water, the size of his body would only have travelled 100 yards or so down-river. "We found nothing," said Altena; "Not a piece of ripped shirt or anything..."

He vanished in a seemingly supernatural speed, practically in plain sight of his father and other relatives. Even mesh fencing strung across the creek yielded nothing. Sheriff Altena chased several leads in an effort to find the little boy. 'Could Breiton have walked the distance of a quarter-mile, to the blacktop highway, and been kidnapped? Could he have fallen into an animal hole and been buried?'

The Sheriff said they gave a polygraph test to a relative who had been at the creek that day. They didn't suspect him, but they wondered, when the man ran off for help and got in his vehicle, could the little boy have snuck inside the vehicle? The relative passed the polygraph though. No-one at the creek is suspected of harming Breiton, Sheriff Altena said. "It's been really hard to never find a body." He said he's still baffled by it and still hoping there will be a clue at some point, that could help locate Breiton.

At the scene where it happened, Altena said, "Just looking at it, you just want to start all over and do a total search all over again, because you think, "How in the world is this possible....?""

On the day he disappeared, the group were all on the small concrete bridge over Willow Creek and said they lost sight of him for less than a minute. Many believed he had to have fallen off the bridge into the creek and drowned, and yet the group of adults and children he was with heard no loud splash, no shout, no scream, no cries. He vanished from among them and they saw nothing....

As the Sheriff says, how is this possible....?

Chapter Three

Missing in the Smoky Mountains

More recently, 'Mystery deepens over missing hiker after body found a week later in Smoky Mountains,' wrote the Charlotte Observer on October 3rd, 2018. A day earlier, search crews had found the body of missing Mitzie Susan Clements under a mile from the Appalachian Trail and approximately two miles from the Clingmans Dome parking area, in the Great Smoky Mountains National Park, North Carolina.

She'd disappeared on September 25th. She'd vanished within a quarter mile of grassy Andrews Bald Mountain, a double peak on the Forney Ridge Trail, just south of Clingman's Dome. 'How she died or how she came to be in that area, was not released,' it was reported.

'The body of a hiker who went missing a week ago in the Great Smoky Mountains National Park has been found; but the mystery grows as to what exactly happened to the 53-year-old mom from Ohio,' said reporter Mark Price.

Mitzie Sue "Susan" Clements was hiking with her daughter when the pair lost sight of each other, according to the National Park Service. This happened at around 5pm after her daughter said she wanted to go on ahead so she could climb the highest point in the Great Smoky Mountains - Clingmans Dome Observation Tower. At an elevation of 6,634, it's the highest point and offers an incredible view of the National Park.

The daughter was going to hike on ahead and would then double back to meet back up with her mother. National Park Officials stated; it was still light and the two were "fairly close to the parking lot. The daughter decided to hike ahead just a little bit," said Parks Spokeswoman Julena Campbell. "The plan was to turn around and just meet up with her. She did that. They weren't separated for very long but when she turned around, she couldn't find her mother."

They were only out for a day hike, and so the mother and her daughter were not dressed for camping at night. The Park Service posted on Facebook. 'Rangers are searching for a 53-year-old woman from Cleves, who was last seen in the Clingman's Dome area, hiking with her daughter on the Fornay Ridge Trail when the two became separated near Andrews Bald. Anyone that saw Clements in the late afternoon or since is asked to call...'

The Charlotte Observer wrote, 'Last seen wearing a green zip-up sweater, black leggings and gray running shoes, the 5'6 missing woman had been expected to meet back with her daughter at the parking lot.' But she never arrived back at the parking area.

The Citizen Times reported that National Parks Spokesperson Julena Campbell told them; "When she (the daughter) arrived at the parking lot, her mother wasn't there." Campbell said, "She waited a little bit, walked around, retraced some of her steps and then called the park."

A search was to begin which would last for a week. Park officials searched the immediate area that night, without success. The next day, a group of experienced searchers spent the night on the Appalachian Trail, attempting to find Clements and also interview any hikers in the area.

More than 100 trained search and rescue personal were brought in to search the "steep rugged terrain" where the missing woman was last seen. The National Park Service website wrote; 'National Park officials have entered the sixth full day of searching. Over the weekend, the search effort intensified with the addition of personnel and specialized equipment from five states. Searchers, canine teams, helicopters and drones are continuing to work in steep, rugged terrain. Around 115 trained searchers and logistical support personnel from dozens of state and local agencies and search and rescue organizations are participating in the search operation led by the National Park Service.'

The search continued to grow in size and scope as personnel withstood heavy rain fog and winds to scour the densely wooded area. 'Thus far searchers have hiked over 500 miles on trails looking for Clements. In addition, canine teams, helicopters, and drones with specialized search and rescue equipment have been used to conduct more intensive off-trail "grid-searches" of approximately 10 square miles.'

Her brother-in-law, a fire-fighter, joined in the search effort. They all found nothing. No sign of the missing woman, no clothes, no personal belongings, no sign of a struggle or injury. 'One week after a woman went missing in the Great Smoky Mountains National Park while hiking with her daughter, national park officials said they still have no clues as to her whereabouts,' said the Citizen Times. Given that it was a very popular hiking trail, in the height of the hiking season and extremely close to the very popular Tourist destination of the look-out tower, how did no-one see her?

Then, on October 3rd, the National Park announced that searchers had found her body at a location two miles west of the parking area she should have been at to meet back up with her daughter. How she died was not released, nor how she came to be in that area.

'The Smokies, which cover a half-million acres, is the most visited national park in the country, with some 11.3 million visitors last year. Usually the busiest month of the year is October, when people come to see the brilliant fall color,' wrote Citizen Times'. How did no-one see her after she disappeared? Why could she not make her way back to the Parking area? What on earth happened to her?

'Cleves woman who went missing while hiking in the Smokies is 11th death in park this year,' says Ashville Citizen. Curiously, it also states 'Clements was found in Great Smoky Mountains National Park after a week of massive searching in terrain so rugged and thick with vegetation a helicopter was needed to extract her.' How was it possible for her to get into that terrain then...?

'While the official cause of death is still under investigation, park spokeswoman Julena Campbell said foul play is not suspected.' The search for Clements lasted a week and involved 175 trained personnel from five states and some 50 organizations, helicopters, drones and K-9 units. It ended when her body was found Tuesday night in "incredibly thick" vegetation in Swain County, 2 miles west of the Clingmans Dome parking lot.

She was just 2 miles from the parking lot. How could they not have found her in that search? Where had she been? What exactly happened to her? And the most curious question of all, how did she get into terrain that was so "incredibly thick" that it needed careful extraction? - in the busiest National Park, in the busiest month of the year, near a very popular tourist spot?

How did no-one see her vanish? How did she vanish, and why? How, if they had searched 500 miles, and "off-grid searches of 10 square miles, could they not have found her? Was she really there all the time....?

Oddly, the exact same trail, Forney Ridge Trail, and the exact same visitor destination Clingman's Dome, was the location for another mysterious disappearance too. Teresa 'Trenny' Lynn Gibson also bizarrely and inexplicably disappeared there too, on October 8th, 1976. 16-year-old Teresa, who was known to her friends and family as 'Trenny,' had gone to the Great Smoky Mountain National Park on a field trip with approximately 30 other students from her high school, Bearden High in Knoxville, Tennessee.

At the time of her disappearance, the school group were hiking a distance of just under 2 miles to reach Bald Mountain from Clingmans Dome and then head back on the Forney Ridge Trail.

As they walked along, the group of 30 or so split off into smaller groups when they reached Forney Ridge Trail. Despite the number of students, they had only 1 teacher accompanying them along with the bus driver. It's understood that Trenny herself spent time with a couple of the separate groups, according to the pace at which she was walking. She was last known to have been seen at approximately 3 pm close to Clingmans Dome on a trail that was quite steep and surrounded by thick woodland on either side of the trail.

At the time of her disappearance, she had been surrounded by the group she was with and other groups of the school party, behind and in front of them, on the same trial. There were also lots of other hikers around too, because of the popularity of the location.

As soon as the Teacher discovered that Trenny was no longer with the rest of the school kids, a search was organized that afternoon, although the weather had turned soggy and rainy and it did hamper the search efforts. Bloodhounds were brought in and her scent was picked up on – where the trail met The Appalachian trail. The bloodhounds followed her scent to Clingmans Dome tower. Her scent stopped near the side of a small road. Had she been abducted?

One possible lead was that back home there'd been an attempted break-in by a young man. Mr Gibson, Trenny's father, had shot him, not fatally, and the young man had issued a threat that he would harm their daughter. However, that lead did not pan out any further than that, according to Knox County P.D.

One theory offered was that perhaps Trenny had been snatched, held at the Tower, which was not searched, and then taken from the scene once the coast was clear, where she was forced into a car at the spot where the dogs lost her scent – where the small road was. A more romantic version is that she planned it herself – to run away and start a new life with someone. But how could she hide or be hidden at such a busy spot of the Tower?

In a retrospective, Wbir News interviewed some of her old classmates and a Ranger involved in the search for her. 'A bus dropped them off that Friday afternoon at Clingmans Dome, one of the most visited spots in the Smokies. The students were to hike down from Clingmans on the Forney Ridge trail about 1.8 miles and then come back. Not that long really.' They saw that Trenny was with a couple of friends who stopped to rest along the trial. 'She went on. And then completely disappeared.'

Although they were only hiking a short distance, the trail had some steep drop-offs. "They were worried about her," said Dwight McCarter, a life-long East Tennessean and retired National Park Ranger who helped hunt for Trenny. "They couldn't figure out what happened to her." Rain and fog had set in as the search for her began. They found no clues, no signs of her.

'The following day,' says Wbir, "about 150 people took part in the search. Again, nothing was found that could offer an explanation about where Trenny was. The next day again, on the Sunday, the search grew in size. Rangers blocked drivers from taking the spur road that leads to Clingmans Dome to prevent the curious getting in the way.

Tracking dogs picked up on Trenny's scent – and that's what puzzles retired Ranger McCarter who took part in dozens of searches during his decade as a ranger. He trusts tracking dogs. Searchers used about a dozen dog teams - bloodhounds, and German shepherds to look for the girl. Three of the dog teams detected Trenny's scent at the intersection with the Appalachian Trail. They followed it by Clingmans Dome. "With all the people at the tower taking in the view," says McCarter, "some of the dogs last detected her scent along the roadside about a mile and a half from Newfound Gap. And that was it..."

The weather prevented an immediate aerial search beginning; because of the bad weather, the helicopters couldn't look for her until later in the afternoon. When they did start to look for her though, they found no signs of her and no clues. The season didn't help. 'Many trees still had their foliage, making it harder to look down onto the ground. The chief ranger told reporters he was almost certain Trenny was not in the Park. But could someone have taken her?'

The FBI went to Trenny's school after she vanished. They interviewed all the students. The investigation went no-where. Myra Bowling had sat at the back of the bus with Trenny that day. Speaking to 10News, she said, "I have never, nor will I ever forget that very long day."

To this day, Trenny has never been found....

Chapter Four

Missing Stacy Arias

'Search halts for woman missing in Yosemite. No sign of 80-year-old hiker found, after eight days scouring the park,' reported The Fresno Bee on August 8th, 2007. 'After looking for 8 days, searchers withdrew on Tuesday.'

The 80-year-old but very fit and very experienced hiker, Ottorrina Bonaventura had disappeared after getting separated from her hiking party in Yosemite National Park. When her family and friends had first heard of her disappearance, they had not immediately become too distressed. They described her as a fitness fanatic who loved a challenge. Every morning she went to the gym, they said, and just a year earlier, at the age of 79 she had ridden a bike across Iowa – a task that took a week.

Her daughter Pam Crnkovich told reporters, "She pushes herself like crazy. She's competitive with herself! Growing up, she was described as a bit of a tomboy. She used to climb mountains," said her daughter. In fact, she travelled internationally to climb in Peru, the Swiss Alps, and Patagonia.

She was a retired computer programmer, and she was not known to be unwell nor on any medication. Although some newspapers claimed she suffered from memory loss, this has since been clarified. Her memory was the same as any 80-year-old, no worse.

On learning of her stamina and fitness and strong character, the Park Ranger search for her had been expanded geographically. "Clearly, this person breaks all expectations of age and physical condition. The more we learned about her, the more respectful we became of her abilities," said Adrienne Freeman, spokesman for Yosemite National Park. In fact, they expanded their search to 100 square miles as a result. Far from fearing the worst, as they began their search, they quickly changed this expectation to one of hopefulness.

31

However, after 8 days of searching passed with no signs of her and no clues about where she could be, they were seriously worried, and their hopes were now fading fast. The missing woman had hiked alone down a trial near Vogelsgang High Camp, and never returned. Over 150 searchers had been joined by helicopters combing the forests, fields and lakes, and the rivers. Parks Spokesperson Freeman said that while the inclination for most lost hikers might be to remain close to where they had got lost, a determined woman such as Bonaventura would probably have pushed on had she become lost.

She was last seen July 30th, when she left her hiking group near Emeric Lake saying that she was going to return to her tent at Vogelsang High Sierra Camp, to check on food storage. This was about 7 miles southeast of Tuolumne Meadows. Park officials were hoping to interview anyone who had been issued with a wilderness permit, in the hope that they might have caught sight of her, as they were desperate for any leads or clues about where she might be. Spokesperson for the National Park, Freeman said individuals had come from throughout the State to join in the search effort, which involved helicopters and search dogs.

On Tuesday August 14th, 15 days later, the body of missing Ottorina Bonaventura was found in the Echo Creek drainage, an area described as a rugged wilderness area southwest of Tuolumne Meadows. Officials announced they had found her deceased in this remote spot after being missing for more than two weeks.

A park ranger who was described as being on a "routine patrol" as opposed to the official search, which had by then been called off, found her body at around 5 pm that afternoon 'in a vegetated area beside a dry creek bed near Echo Creek, just 3 miles from her campground by air,' but in a spot that is 'unreachable via established trails,' said spokesperson Adrienee Freeman.

"It's just such a huge rugged area and searching is very difficult out there," she added. She said that the coroner's office would determine cause of death but that the Park service did not believe there was any foul play. Despite her fitness, and determined nature, one has to ask, how could she end up in a spot "unreachable via trails" and why...?

Close-by, a girl by the name of Stacy Arias also disappeared. Archive files from the National Park Service in 1981 describe what happened. 'Last seen, she was wearing a white windbreaker, light coloured short sleeve blouse, shorts, grey hiking boots size 8 or 9, gold ankle bracelet, 5'5 tall, 120 lbs.'

On the missing person's poster, it highlights her vulnerability; 'When her blonde hair is combed forward, she looks 16 years old, and when her hair is pulled back in a ponytail, she looks 12 years old. When last seen, wearing an off-white, pullover windbreaker, with horizontal zipper front pouch above breast-line and a hood that hangs down the back or tucks inside. She is wearing upper and lower narrow teeth retainers. She may be carrying a small Olympus camera with embroidered neck strap, multi-coloured, predominantly black. She may also be carrying cigarettes and gum.'

Stacy Arias was on a horse-riding trip with her father, George, and seven others, in the Sunrise Meadows area of the Yosemite National Park, in California. It was July 17th, 1981. After they'd been riding for a few hours, the group stopped at cabins at the Sunrise High Sierra Camp, a small site with 8 other cabins and located approximately one and a half miles from Sunrise Lakes. It's the last camp before the end of the High Sierra Loop. Here, they climbed off the horses and were going to have some refreshments and then stay there for the night. The cabins overlook a meadow. After refreshments and a change of clothes, Stacy set off with her camera to take photos of the Lake. She was never seen again.

She'd apparently asked her dad if he wanted to go with her, but he had declined, and instead, a 72-year-old man who was travelling with them accompanied her. They walked off together, but after a short while the man became tired and so he sat down to take a rest while Stacy continued onward to the Lake. The others back at the Cabin had watched the pair as they set off and they later recalled that they saw the elderly man sit down to take a rest.

The group said they continued to watch Stacy walking down the hill herself until she disappeared from view as a couple of trees blocked their sight of her. She remained out of sight after that, but the watchers were not concerned at that point – it was natural she would disappear from their view due to the landscape now coming between them.

There are conflicting reports; the Fresno Bee says the man was 77 and he walked with Stacy for at least 20 minutes away from the camp before stopping – a further distance than other reports say.

The elderly man sat and waited for some time her to return from the Lake and when she didn't, he started to grow a little concerned, and he returned to the camp to ask the rest of the group to go with him to bring her back to camp. Among the trees she had walked into, they discovered the lens cap of her camera. In the trees and at the Lake, there was no sign of Stacy however.

She did not return to camp that evening, said National Park Service Spokeswoman Sharon Johnson, at the time. Over the next few days, hundreds of searchers, including the National Guard, scoured the area between the Camp and the Lake. No clues were found about where she could be.

Eight members of CLMRP, China Lake Mountain Rescue Group joined the search on July 23rd, at Base Camp run by Park Ranger Durr and Joint Operation Leader Miner Harkness of Sierra Madre. 'Not a shred of evidence of Stacy was discovered,' they wrote in their report. Then the McLatchley News Service said; 'The search for Stacy Arias who disappeared in the Yosemite High County 11 days go has been called off."

The Saratoga teenager "Just seems to have disappeared," said National Park Service Superintendent Robert O. Binneweis. Volunteers and Rangers had logged thousands of hours searching for her.

Her disappearance became a mystery. Some people felt the teenage girl may have 'taken a walk,' and that unless she did walk off intentionally, hopes of finding her alive now were considered slim, said Rangers. Parks spokeswoman Linda Abbott said the girl's last talk with her father was over footwear. She was wearing thongs until her father told her she should be wearing hiking boots if she planned to walk away to take pictures. "If she had planned on walking off, she wouldn't have gone off in thongs," said the parks spokeswoman.

'The lack of the usual summer thunderstorm,' said the McLatchley News, 'may have hampered the search, rangers said. Dog teams brought into the area were unable to pick up any scent because of the dry and dusty conditions.'

In the National Park Service archives, Chief Ranger Charles W. Wendt's report of 23rd July 1981 states; 'The air operations for the Stacy Arias search began in earnest on Saturday July 18th.' There is also a letter sent from National Park Service Superintendent Robert O. Binneweis to Dave McCoy of the Mammoth Mountain Ski Area Resort, thanking his organisations for help in the search efforts; 'Although the search was unsuccessful and not a single clue was found, we feel that Stacy had the best possible chance due to the professional efforts of organisations such as yours.'

It appears that Superintendent Binneweis also sent similar letters, to among others, Riverside Mountain Rescue Unit of California, Malibu Search and Rescue, Air National Guard, Scott Air Force Base of Illinois. Clearly then, the search for Stacy was incredibly thorough.

San Jose Search and Rescue, dressed in orange jumpsuits, scaled down ravines on climbing ropes and searched drainage creeks, for spots where a body could be lying hidden. Park officials said it was possible the girl had hiked to a road and left the park. "I can tell you that they have not turned up anything," said Parks Spokeswoman Linda Abbott.

According to the Mariposa Gazette, the 77-year-old man who had accompanied her and then stopped to sit down while she continued, told Park officials that he had spoken to a group of people coming from the direction that Stacy had taken, but that they had not seen the girl. It seems that Stacy Arias disappeared among the trees in an area very popular with hikers. Only her camera lens cap was left. How could she simply vanish like this? The spot in which she disappeared is very close to a highway that runs parallel; a distance of a kilometre away. Searchers found no signs of any struggle, no signs of violence – just the lens cap of her camera. Did one of the other hikers in the area come across this teenage girl, who the NPS missing posters described as sometimes looking like a vulnerable 11-year-old? Did they snatch her fast, without being seen, and manage to get her to the highway before anyone saw them? - Although that would have required not being seen for a kilometre.

Or was she hidden in a tent nearby? And yet surely this would have been very hard to do successfully in an area so popular with visitors? Had the serial killer Carl Stayner found her easy prey? – He had been known to visit Yosemite and had indeed abducted and killed several women in Yosemite National Park; 'After four brutal murders, a number of false leads and a growing sense of panic in one of California's most celebrated beauty spots, police and federal agents are at last confident that they have cracked the case of a serial killer stalking the state's Yosemite National Park,' wrote the Independent, when Carl Stayner was eventually caught.

In 1999, a serial killer was roaming Yosemite National Park, in California's Sierra Nevada Mountains. It began when a letter was sent to the police, along with a hand-drawn map. The letter said, "We had fun with this one." The map indicated a location where a body had been dumped.

The police went to the location on the home-made map and there they found a body. It was a young woman. Her throat had been slashed so savagely that her head was severed. Her killer took her head with him. He later confessed that he was intending to keep it as a trophy, but then decided to through it into a pool of water instead. The killer's name was Carl Stayner and his own brother had once been abducted and held for years by a child predator.

Stayner was employed by the National Park Service. His victim was Julie Sund and she'd gone missing in the

National Park. Search and Rescue had looked extensively for her with dogs. The FBI were called in when her purse was found in Modesto. She'd been abducted from outside of her cabin and she was at least his 4th victim.

"Our visitors leave the urban areas thinking they are getting away from all that, [but) they are being followed into the parks by professional criminals," said Ranger Joe Smith in the National Park Service's division of law enforcement, in Washington, D.C. to the Sun Sentinel in 1994.

Between 1988 and 1992, the National Park Service reported 104 homicides and 393 rapes in its 365 parks. During 2006, 11 deaths were investigated across the system. Two involved women who had been pushed off cliffs - one at Pictured Rocks National Lakeshore on the southern shore of Lake Superior, and the other at Golden Gate National Recreation Area.

Ocala National Forest was where hitchhiker, prostitute and serial killer Aileen Wournos disposed of a victim's body. And it was 6 miles from there in the same national park that honors student John Timothy Edwards from Florida State University, was murdered and his 21-year-old sister raped twice and tied to a tree. In 1988, a girl and her boyfriend were killed in the woods.

On Thanksgiving in 1992, hunters in the Big Scrub area of Ocala National Forest discovered the skeletal remains of Retha Hanna, a 25-year-old from Leesburg, thought to have been the victim of a serial killer. In 1985, the body of Susan Jo Lazarus was found in the woods after going missing. She had been shot with the gun she carried for own protection.

One of the most notorious still unsolved murders in Ocala National Forest is that of the 1966 killings of Pamela Nater, 20, and Nancy Leichner, 21, who disappeared while on a youth trip in the Alexander Springs Recreation Area of the Forest. It is thought that Policeman-turned-Serial-killer Gerard J. Schaefer was possibly their killer. Pamela, Nancy and their boyfriends were hanging out at the Lake. Their boyfriends, who had been in the water, found Nancy's glasses and the girls' purses and shoes at a picnic table they'd been sitting at when they returned to shore, but their girlfriends had vanished. There was no trace of either of the women.

Nancy was reportedly last seen on a nearby nature trail; a long narrow and winding path that follows the Alexander Spring Creek, at approximately 12.30 pm. Pam was reportedly last seen about an hour after that, a short distance from the same trail.

A jailhouse confession along with eyewitness reports would later indicate that former cop Gerard J. Schaefer had abducted and killed the two women. While in prison, he told a cellmate that he snatched them by threatening them with a gun and knife. He also wrote a letter to a former girlfriend confessing to their forest killings.

Witness Brant Hoover, who was 11 years old at the time and in a canoe on the lake that day, said he was certain he saw Schaefer following the two girls before they were abducted. Their bodies however have never been found.

In February 1973, four teenage boys, 19-year-old Brian Scott Card, 18-year-old Robert Spector, 18-year-old David Olicker, and 15-year-old Mark Dreibelbis were camping in Henry Cowell Redwoods State Park in California. They fashioned a home-made cabin and set about enjoying themselves. Sometime later, a man approached them.

The man told them that he was a Park Ranger and they must pull down their make-shift cabin and leave the area. The boys refused to do this. They did not believe they were doing anything wrong. They ignored him and carried on with what they were doing. In turn, the man who said he was a Park Ranger, stormed off; telling them he would be back the next day.

Sure enough, the next day, he returned. Again, he pretended to be a Park Ranger; what the boys could never have known was that really, he was a schizophrenic serial killer who had already killed eight people. His name was Herbert Mullin. He shot them all dead at point blank range. It was a week before their bodies were discovered. He said he had no choice; he said he had to do it because if he didn't an earthquake would happen, and it would kill everyone!

Chapter Five

Secret Bases & The Missing

But can Serial Killers be blamed for the many hundreds of people who have disappeared and continue to disappear in wilderness areas...in the blink of an eye...?

Sweet Grass County Sheriff's Lieutenant Ronneberg said, during the search for missing hunter Aaron Hedges; "All theories have been thought up, everything from he got turned around off the trail, passed away from hypothermia, to he's in Mexico somewhere, to UFOs got him." And, in the case of the missing Park Ranger, his father said, "It was like a UFO sucked him up...." So, are 'the missing' snatched by serial killers, or is there something even more terrifying going on...?

Well, a man called Aaron Egan McCollum claims to have been part of a black-ops MILAB group who are responsible for snatching targets, male and female, children too, to underground bases for experimentation and programming, in league with ET's. He talks about the retrieval of renegade agents, where the programming has malfunctioned, and of targets being returned with no knowledge they have been taken, or worse, terminated.

He claims to have been at several secret underground bases, which have an ET presence, and that as a child, he was taken to some of these facilities to be trained in an MK Ultra style of sensory deprivation specifically underwater.

Not only does his story of snatching targets make me think of the many people missing from national parks, woods and forests, gone in the blink of an eye; but also of the many missing college-age men who have disappeared, and of course, this alleged whistleblower's initiation and training underwater also brings to mind that many of these young men are later found dead in water. Could a MILAB-style secret program be behind some of these disappearances?

This is his abridged story, as told to Project Camelot. True or fantasy? Before we begin, perhaps the rational minded of us would question his claim of knowing other 'super-soldiers' who have come out over the years, all claiming forced involvement in secret black operations and ET and mind control and rituals and global elite agendas; Are any of these 'super-soldiers' credible? Or are they all telling tall-tales? Although perhaps in their defence, maybe some of them are genuine, and maybe they are looking for others who say they too have had the same experiences, to try to make sense of what they have been through themselves – things that if true, have been so traumatic it has shattered their psyche's, and fractured their minds.

McCollum claims he was in the US Coast Guards for 10 years and involved in 'Black Ops' projects separate to the Coast Guards. "Things you see in the movies are put there as a ruse to automatically give this the label of "Sci-fi, fantasy" so people will not dig in anymore and they'll live in their world of "it's just make-believe."

He claims to have worked in a 'special ops' team within

'Project Talent.' "The project has two sides – the people that were never in the Military; civilians, but who worked directly in the military – sometimes they would even wear military uniforms. Then people like me. I did not choose the branch of service I was to go in; certain individuals, agents, came to me and told me which branch I was going in. I got regular training but at times I would be temporarily assigned to other units. I wasn't doing what was known by my commanding officer – there was no name, no denomination of rank, no i.d., nothing. It was 'Umbrella operations.' It was increasing the training that I had started when I was very young. It's fuzzy. I've been regaining memories of back in 2008. There is a research company that deals specifically in genetics and DNA, specifically alien/human DNA. In a base, underwater. There's a lot of underwater bases.

In 2008, I was approached by a Captain in the Marine's Intelligence. I met with this gentleman and several others who I am not quite sure who they worked for - several were Australian. We started doing a lot of Stateside projects. With every underground base, there is at least some presence of ET's. But I will tell you; none of them are friendly. They're really running the show."

Project Seagate involved an underground base located in Puerto Rico – this is the one I have recovered memories about. I have probably regained 40% of my memories. Why is this happening? I don't know. Unfortunately, there are times when I still get triggered and am taken elsewhere to do things – as recently as a couple of months ago, when I have 2 days I cannot account for.

With Project Seagate, I found out that frequencies are used to put you on a molecular level into a different state. This way, your body can handle travelling great distances – you get aligned to the same frequency as a dolphin; that this heightens the human awareness. One of the things they did was part of "Psychic echo-location." It has to be people that have received certain training and with some amount of psychic ability. They learned that they could put a person in with these dolphins and actually it would cause deep molecular and psychic vibrations to happen, and the dolphin is almost used as a medium, and this person becomes a conductor, and this really heightens the psyche of a person."

"Project Seagate was a major project with a huge underground base location, and they were working on many different sub-projects; it's almost like a sub – version of MK Ultra. One location; many different sub-projects, everything from the human-dolphin programme to an Omega programme where they were making soul-less beings for remote viewing and actually via the Seagate, being able to put people, and yes, that's real people - their astral self, their energy, their souls, into one of these robots for covert operations. I have people that I know this has happened to and we have absolute evidence of this happening."

"The place we lived in, in Oregon, when I was 3, we had a military facility that was nearby. I don't remember much of it, but it was a place that my father worked at. He wasn't in the military, but he worked there at the time. I wasn't taken there by my father, but I was taken there by someone and then I would be taken to this house with this gentleman that I know was much older – I've got confirmation of this from my sister. At this house, I was put through various things; one of the things I remember, it wasn't a closet, but it was a constructed compartment, soundproofed pitch black."

"As far as alterations done to my body - even as a child. My body has been through a living hell. I had some questionable experimentations that were done to me as a child that I absolutely remember. I have an absolute memory that I have been able to get confirmed from family, where I was taken to a facility by a certain relative when I was 3 years old and thrown into a pool, and they induced me to drown."

"I remember laying then on a slab next to the pool, throwing up and coughing up water and then seeing these men around me saying; "We have one." I remember hearing that. I still wake up having night terrors and flashbacks about this. And a sound-proofed pitch-black room. I was put in there for hours at a time. It was, what I've discovered now, you could say, a sensory deprivation chamber. Now, imagine what that's like, being a child. I imagine I was afraid."

"I don't really recognize or even understand that emotion of fear now. There were a lot of emotions that were taken out of me. I almost mimic emotions now in a way; I've had to, to fit into the world. It was sensory and pain training; but I remember other things too – of being with a group of kids and being taken to what I know now is referred to as 'The Camps.' It could be for a week to several weeks. Survival training, hand to hand combat, from age 5-8."

"There are times I remember at the camps having to learn to go out on the land and survive. I remember being forcibly dunked for a week, over and over again into water submersion, and of being subjected to violence; of being numb to it. I was taken to a place with about a dozen other kids, the same kids. We were taken to this dug-out. They called it 'The Pit.' We had to fight. It was about 8 years later I remember some girls integrated into this training. These training facilities are located all over the country."

He says he carried out Military abductions. "Let's say you've got a Remote Viewer, who was part of one of the sub-projects in MK Ultra, brought up into it as I was, or a scientist – but they defect; their programming has broken down and they don't want to be part of it anymore, so the team I was with do one of two things; we either terminate the subject or we bring them back for reprogramming/military abduction. That's just one of the many reasons for an abduction. Sometimes it was children, there was a lot of variety."

"When I was doing these military abductions, they were brought back to a designated installation, sometimes it was underground, sometimes it was an above secret installation, sometimes a military base. One of the places was an underground facility in the Northern bay of San Francisco. Black triangle craft were used a lot. The sound of it could be altered so if its really dark out you see lights that appear to be a 747 and appear like a 747 but there's always that chance it could be a black triangle." (ie he means it is disguised somehow.)

"They may not be gone forever (the targets) – they're called 'Subjects of opportunity.' We were working with ET's. Plain daylight abductions, where you could be masked like a priest and you draw them into a situation and grab them. We would use several different drugs – one of them was called scopamine. With Scopamine I can literally take it and get it on the end of a toothpick and let's say I've tracked you down – you're at a café. I can wait until you go to the bathroom, put some in your coffee, or just put some on your skin, wait for it to take effect. Then I walk over to you and say, "Come with Me," and you come – this is how it works, you grab your purse and you come with me, willingly. We take you to a facility. If you are returned, you will have no memories of what was done to you. That's what the drug does – it's a very dangerous drug, and one of the drugs of choice for our abductions, GBH too. I did have two females on my team."

Now this reminds me of the abducted college-age men; so many who have vanished on a night out, while in the company of their friends, and never been seen again. It's been going on for so many years too.

As I've been writing, since my first book in 2014 in 'Mysterious things in the Woods,' and in most of my books after this, about the strange water deaths of young men in both rural and urban areas, it is a disturbing and horrifying enigma, that seems to continue unabated and unchallenged. Is it a supernatural mystery, or urbane and completely explainable, or is it an organised practice that harks back to ancient occult sacrifice? – For more detailed cases and investigations, please see my books 'An investigation into the Smiley Face Killers,' or 'Dead in the Water.'

It's something I've been researching now since about 2013 and I've been given some very troubling possible answers to the causes of young men disappearing and being found dead later in water, and some of these answers are no doubt correct; but for now, I cannot reveal them and perhaps I too am being hoodwinked; perhaps.

Could any of these cases be as a result of MILAB-style abductions, as the whistle-blower claims; dosed with scopamine in a bar and abducted to a clandestine base for experimentation....?

'River death teenager James Corfield did NOT drown, inquest told,' despite him being found dead in the river. Pathologist said there was no evidence of assault or drowning - leaving investigators in a difficult position,' reported Wales Online. The authorities admitted they had a mystery on their hands.

'James Corfield did not drown, also said the Coroner. The coroner, as well as the medical examiner could find no other cause of death either. James Corfield's case is eerily similar to the many cases presented in my 'Investigation into the Smiley Face Killers' book and 'Dead in the Water,' book, which describe case after case of student-aged men disappearing on a night-out, not being found for some time, and then mysteriously being found dead in water, but often it is water they have not drowned in. James Cornfield unexplained disappearance is just like theirs.

19-year-old James Corfield was reported missing after leaving the White Horse pub in Builth Wells, in the county of Powys, Brecknockshire, in mid Wales, on Monday 24th July 2017. He was attending the Royal Wales Agricultural Show nearby. He was last seen on council CCTV footage crossing the Grove Car Park in the Market town of Builth Wells at 11.56 pm. He was found dead in 3 feet of water in the River Wye five days later. How do you drown in 3 feet of water?

He'd been seen earlier in the evening at the show's Member's bar on CCTV, then on a minibus into town, and he was last seen at 11.56 pm when he walked across a car park in Builth Wells, having left the White Horse Pub. The alarm was raised at around 2pm the following day when he failed to meet his parents as arranged. His body was found five days later but an inquest into his death heard that the post-mortem examination carried out on his body found no direct evidence that he had drowned, and the conclusion was that his death was a mystery.

"We are left in the difficult situation that James has been recovered from water and there is no concrete evidence from the post-mortem examination that he has drowned," said Forensic Pathologist Richard Jones. The pathologist added that there was no evidence of assault or restraint. He told the Inquest that he therefore could not give a cause of death based on medical probabilities. He suggested that James may have died from the physical effects of being suddenly immersed in cold water.

Although he was last seen on CCTV at 11.55 pm, witness statements from friends describe later sightings of him. During the inquest, statements were read out from people who had seen him. A friend of the family, Sain Roberts said she had seen him at a marquee outside the White Horse pub at around 12.30 am. "It was at that time I saw James. He walked past but he stopped to talk to us. He seemed merry." Another witness, Fraser Moss said, "I was with James at the Marquee at around 1 am. We were chatting and dancing. He was drunk but in control." Elliot Clifton said, "James was there on his own. I bought him a drink. He appeared his normal self. He was drunk but coherent. I didn't have any concerns for him."

Earlier that day, young farmer James had met up with his parents at the Royal Welsh Show. It was a Show he'd gone to every year. "A visit to the Show was a real treat for him – and seeing the sheep and poultry judging was something he really looked forward to," said his mother. "He went to the Show every year throughout his life and we have fond memories of taking him as a child." The Royal Welsh Show is a popular annual agricultural event where prize farm livestock are exhibited along with food and craft stalls, and a wide range of activities such as forestry, horticulture, and outdoor sports such as pole climbing and wood stocking competitions. It's held from the 22nd to 25th July each year at the showground in Llanelwedd, Builth Wells.

James had a known passion for farming and had set up his own business selling eggs to local businesses. As a teenager, he had his own sheep and cattle. His mother said farming was his life and he loved his animals with a passion. At the inquest, he was described as an extremely talented young man, excelling in both sports and academically, with a strong entrepreneurial spirit. He was also a keen and talented cricketer. "A genuinely fast bowler and attacking batsman, his talents made him the Shropshire Division Two Cricketer of the Year and the League's Young Player of the Year in 2016. So successful was James last year that we joked with the family that they would need extra shelves to show off all his trophies. "His parents said he smiled all the time. His mother told the Inquest that he disappeared on the first time he had stayed away from home. When his parents met him at the Show, his mother said the first thing he said to her was, "I'll be back in the morning."

The Inquest at Welshpool Magistrates Court heard that James had been camping with friends at the show. Initially, his disappearance was treated as "Low risk" according to Police Inspector Andrew Pitt, who led the search. However, after interviews with his friends failed to reveal where he was, the case was upgraded. Residents living nearby were urged to check their garden sheds and other outbuildings for signs of James.

After his disappearance, his parents said, "This is totally out of character of James. He is so passionate about his farm animals and hasn't come home to them. He would never leave them unattended, which makes us even more worried about where he is. James is a gifted cricket player, and is due to play cricket this Saturday, and his team, Montgomery Cricket Club, need him home for this. We still can't find him and need your help. Where is he?"

He was last seen wearing a royal blue Abercrombie polo shirt with a white logo, dark blue jeans and light brown deck shoes. Hundreds of volunteers signed up for a police register to help look for him and groups of up to 50 staff from the Welsh Show and police officers scoured the area around the Young Peoples Village, about a mile north of the showground, where James was camping with friends. The next day, over 100 volunteers searched the area around the Young Peoples Village.

CCTV pictures of Mr Corfield's last known movements were played at the inquest in Welshpool. It showed him walking away from a group of minibuses for people staying at the young people's village across the River Wye from the main showground. He was seen heading in the direction of the rugby field which has a path alongside the river.

The initial search took place at the river because of its proximity to the bar. West Wales Fire and Rescue Service, Brecon Mountain Rescue specialist water search, and rescue volunteers were using inflatable boats in the search. Superintendent Jon Cummins asked people to stay away from the search area in order that specially trained officers and rescue teams could carry out their work. Search dogs, mountain rescue teams, divers and boat teams and the police were joined in their search by hundreds of volunteers.

A spokesman said: "Whilst river levels are low, there are sections of fast-moving water, deep pools and unstable banks, so members of the public are asked to keep themselves safe and stay away from the river.A police helicopter, along with boat and dive teams, mountain rescue crews, the fire service and search dog handlers were involved, along with other volunteers.

His parents said his disappearance was "totally out of character." His mother told a police family liaison officer her son "Would not have gone into the river voluntarily" as he did not like the water. When his body was found five days later, the Inspector said there was "no credible information" of any third-party involvement and no evidence of foul play, no evidence of an assault. On the CCTV as he walks across the car park having left the pub, three men were seen walking behind him. Police said they did not believe the men had anything to do with James' disappearance though.

James' blood alcohol level was above the drink-drive limit, but not extreme. His body was found submerged in the river Wye by divers on July 30th near the confluence of the Rivers Wye and Irfon, in 3ft of water. "The only thing I can say for certain is that James hasn't entered the river from a lower point from where he'd been found," said Inspector Pitt. Asked why it took so long to find him, the Inspector said he believed the young man's body may have been in a deep pool near the confluence of the rivers before moving into the shallower water, where it was found.

"I believe the most likely scenario is that he had tried to cross the river where the rivers Wy and Irfon meet, possibly realizing that he was on the wrong side (of the river)," said the Inspector. James would have been able to see the lights and hear music from the Young People's Village at the time he entered the water, said the local Newspaper.

His mother however, finds this theory unacceptable. "That wasn't him," she told the Inquest. She said she did not believe her son would ever have voluntarily entered the water. "It was not James. He would never have entered the water willingly."

'Dr. Jones said there was no evidence about whether Mr Corfield had died in the water or out of it, or from any heart condition and he could not give a medical cause of death. The Police inspector hypothesized that he died as a result of jumping in the river to swim across it to his campsite. Is this really something a person would do, rather than arriving at the campsite in a more traditional manner? Would it really be the first thing you would think of doing? The young man has never been described as an adrenaline junkie nor a risk taker, but he was described as disliking water; so why would he even consider the idea of jumping in and swimming?

Dyfed-Powys Police Inspector Pitt said he believed James had entered the river around half a mile from the site of the Young People's Village at the Show. He said James' body was found in three feet of water around 15 metres from the river bank. He described the area as having a shallow bank with a "sudden drop" in the water at around five metres away from the bank. Inspector Pitt said he believed James' body had moved from the point where he entered the water. He said: "The area he was found was only three feet deep and had he been there the whole time I would have expected him to be found there."

The post-mortem examination found no direct evidence that he had drowned and that his medical cause of death remained a mystery. Coroner Andrew Barkley said he believed James died in the water although Dr Jones said there was no evidence about whether James had died in the water or out of it, or from any heart condition, and he could not give a medical cause of death, and his death occurred in circumstances that were not clear. The Coroner said it was possible he decided to cross the river. His family however, vehemently denied this was a possibility, or that he stumbled and fell in.

The inquest heard that while he was followed by three males there appeared to be no interaction between them as Mr Corfield crossed the car park in the direction of a footpath along the river. "I'm afraid I, or anyone else, cannot give the family the answers they so desperately seek," said the Coroner.

How was it that he wasn't found for a week with hundreds of people searching such a small area? What was the time of death? Was it on the night he disappeared or sometime after that? If so, what was he doing in the interim? And why did he end up dead in the water, with no cause of death... when he hated water?

In this next case, an hour and a half away, in Worcester, England, the Birmingham Mail writes; 'Young man's best friend says, "He vanished in 2 minutes!"

His best friend, Harley Hetherington left the Nightclub before him. Harley left somewhere between 2 am and 2. 30 am and half an hour before his friend Thomas, who then mysteriously vanished. Described as "a gentle boy," Thomas Jones is believed to have been close to home when he disappeared. 5ft 5" and of slim build, Thomas had just started his Freshman year at University. In fact, he hadn't even attended his first lecture yet. On the night he disappeared, he phoned his new flatmate to tell him he was "two minutes from home".

Prior to this, he had gone to MacDonald's by Foregate Street Train Station. Between 3 am and 3.40 am, the local Newspaper reported that his mother received a phone call from him, telling her that he was back at his flat – although actually, he was not – he was still out. Perhaps he told her he was back home at the student accommodation so that she didn't stay awake all night worrying about him being out, as many parents tend to do.

Harley Hetherington, his best friend, said that at the time of Thomas' disappearance, he was "in high spirits" enjoying this "new chapter" in his life, starting university, just hours before he vanished. Harley had been one of the last to see his friend, in Velvet Nightclub, Worcester. Harley had gone to school with Thomas, whose nickname is "Jonah," and they'd both enrolled on the same teaching degree course at Worcester Uni. The night Thomas disappeared, he and Harley had originally arranged to meet at midnight at a Wetherspoon's pub, but as it was shut, they met in the nightclub instead, and this was the last time Harley saw Thomas, his friend since age 9.

"When he got to the club, he was going to meet some other people. As he went off, I was with my flatmates. I saw him again about half an hour later on his own, having fun dancing, like anyone does in a nightclub. I went to leave, and I asked him if he'd be ok getting back, and he said he was waiting for somebody and then he'd be off. He told me and a few others on the night, that he was with somebody, but no-one knows who, and CCTV footage suggests he might not have been."

As has very often been the case, men who have disappeared on a night out in the UK, Ireland, US and Canada as first identified by Retired Detective NYPD Kevin Ganon and partner, unidentified people have been in the vicinity. Nothing strange in that really; after all, they are out in the town socializing like hundreds of other young people. Why not go off with strangers if they'd invited him to a party, for example, or told him about a good late-night bar, let's say. In Thomas' case perhaps they'd met a female student or met someone on the internet or through a dating app, but didn't want to go into details about it in case it didn't work out with his date? But is there any chance that some of these unidentified people could be playing a role in the baffling disappearances and deaths of these young men? Not on a random basis, but in a way that is more sinisterly organized? – for further investigation into this please see my 'Investigation into The Smiley Face Killers' and 'Dead in the Water' books.

"He might have been with someone or waiting to meet someone at some point; we just don't know, but he was happy to be there, he was loving it," says Harley. At

3.30 am, we know that Thomas phoned his flatmate (in student accommodation) to tell him he was "Two minutes away." 'At 3.40 am he put a photo of himself by Worcester Race Course on Snapchat,' reported the local Newspaper. However, his friends and family in the Facebook group set up to try to find him, dispute this and say, this did not happen. Of course, Snapchat messages are designed to 'self-destruct' and so it wouldn't be possible to find that message now, to prove or disprove it. If he had sent it, had it been a Selfie that he took himself, alone? Or, could someone have taken it of him? Could someone else have been with him? Could they have sent it (if it was sent) as a twisted taunt perhaps?

At 3.44 am, he phoned his flatmates, and at 3. 46 am he messaged one of his flatmates. At 3.48 am, one of his flatmates called him – but Thomas's phone didn't ring. The call would not go through. Had his phone gone dead? Had his battery died? Or had someone switched off his phone? Again, his case is eerily similar to the case of many other students who have been found mysteriously dead in rivers after vanishing on a night out. Could some of them be tragic drinking accidents? Certainly, but are they all? And why do their phones often go dead?

His best friend Harley told newspapers he'd heard that Thomas's phone had a low battery at this point, and that is very possible with iPhones, but Harley believes that what happened in those two minutes, between the time when Thomas sent a message on his phone to one of his flatmates, and when one of his flatmates tried to call him back, could be of critical importance. Harley said he believed its unlikely his friend's phone simply cut off.

"Logically thinking, from 3.46 to 3.48 am; that's when he went missing. It's a 2-minute time period. From my perspective, I can't see how you can go missing in that time. People don't just vanish," Harley told newspapers. But from my research, they do, and on a chillingly regular basis, if they are college aged and male. "The only thing I can think is he's ended up in the river or he's been taken by someone," said Harley. But, it could be both.

Three days later, the missing young man's parents said there was a possible sighting of Thomas, looking dazed and asking for directions to the City Centre, three days after he disappeared. His father, Ian Jones, said a woman had seen the missing person's posters of his son and said that she had seen him around 2.30 am that day. His parents said, that from looking at the CCTV footage, they were "80% certain" this was their missing son.

The police said they believed that on the night Thomas disappeared, he had crossed the Sabrina footbridge, which crosses the River Severn close to Worcester Racecourse (where it had been said but also disputed that Thomas had sent the snapchat picture of himself.) And they believe he had then walked onto the footpath that runs along the top of the flood defence in Hylton Road — the direction of Hallow, where his accommodation was, just before 3.50 am. This is a route commonly used by students who are returning from Worcester town centre to the University where their dorms are. Since then, he had not been heard from or seen since.

His aunt, Jackie Rogers, said a "small army" was carrying out house- to- house enquiries in and around Hylton Road area to "find our boy." The search for missing Thomas involved "Hundreds of police officers." His best friend made it clear that Thomas "is not a person ready to give up on life. He was excited to go to Uni and was excited to be with people. It's an environment we had all been craving, surrounded by people the same age and fun." His friends all described him as "Popular "outgoing" "funny" and "always with people," and a person who was "fun to be around." He loved being with others, having fun, they all said. 25,000 missing person's posters were handed out; close to the number of people who joined his Facebook page 'Find Johnas.'

Trained specialist teams were brought in and his wide circle of friends and family all searched everywhere for him. Police carried out extensive enquiries including large scale CCTV and phone work. His parents viewed more CCTV in the interim. "We've looked at more footage which we are 80% certain is Thomas that's got across the river. He said he was 2 minutes way, which makes sense. He probably was 2 minutes away – we need to know what's happened from there – because he just disappeared."

Police dive teams conducted searches. West Mercia Search and Rescue searched the river. Hundreds of volunteers joined the police, and police officers worked around the clock trying to find him. "It was full and thorough searches," said Detective Inspector Mark Bellamy. The police had been in the river for days, looking in case he had gone downstream. Then, police announced they had found his body. "Officers searching for missing student Thomas Jones have found a body in the River Servern.'

His best friend said, on the night he vanished, Thomas was "Behaving normally. He didn't seem intoxicated at all." He was just "his usual bubbly self," he said. "You can tell when somebody has had a few; but Thomas wasn't like that – there was no sign of drink or drugs – and that's what has baffled us all. It was just like talking to him at a lecture in the middle of the day – that's how little he'd had to drink. Nobody can quite understand how its happened. He was close to getting home safe and had told people he was fine right up until the point he was missing."

His body was found in the river near Browns restaurant at the Quay in the city centre. A police cordon was erected between Browns and the Worcestershire County Cricket Club. What's never been explained, is how he somehow disappeared in 2 minutes....

His death is being treated by police as "Unexplained."

~~~

Albert Burtoo was a former soldier who had served in the Queen's Royal Regiment from 1924, and during World War Two he had been in the Hampshire Regiment. After the war, he emigrated to Canada where he lived in the wild and hunted bears. When he returned to England, he became a farmer and an avid fisherman and lover of history. One thing he was not interested in was sci-fi or aliens. However, little did he know that when he was 78, they would come for him.

On the night it happened, he had spent the evening along Basingstoke canal, just off Government Road in Aldershot, Hampshire, England. He was night fishing. It was August 12th, 1983, and he had his dog with him. It was calm and tranquil as usual, and he was very relaxed as he sat beside the river. What roused him however was a sudden bright white light coming closer from a distance in the sky. It appeared to be moving and was travelling at an astonishing speed; right in his direction. There were few stars out that night and the dark sky was very clear, which was why it stood out even more so.

He couldn't take his eyes off the fast-moving light until, to his horror, it stopped directly above where he sat. Then it came down, in a field along the river. At first, he assumed it had to be a military craft, as the Ministry of Defence had a base close-by and Aldershot is known for its large military training base. He thought it had to have come down as an emergency landing, but he had heard no crash nor saw any flames and so he settled back down to his fishing once more.

After a few minutes however, his dog began to become very restless, standing up and pacing and it began to whine. His dog was usually very quiet when they were fishing, and not accustomed to whining and so this perturbed him. He tried to calm the dog down, and as he was doing so he noticed that something was moving in the direction of where the bright white light had landed.

As they came closer, he realized that it was figures moving in the darkness, and there were two of them. They appeared to be green in colour. It looked like two men, but they were clothed from head to toe in green. They had visors over their eyes, which were also green, but he could not see their eyes.

At this point, being a former soldier and bear-hunter, and despite the oddity of their appearance, he did not feel afraid. The beings gestured to him, beckoning him to them. He later said, that with his life's experiences and being of an old age now, he felt he had nothing to fear from them and he willingly went to them. He said that they took him to where the white light had landed, and he saw a craft had landed there. "They just stopped and looked at me and I did the same," he later said.

They gestured for him to join them inside and again he went with them. "We walked along the towpath till we reached the railings by the canal bridge." The Beings in front of him, he said, went through the railings on the river path "just like a ghost" while he himself had to climb over the top of the railings. The three of them then crossed Government Road, to reach the downed craft.

Once inside the mysterious object, he said he found himself immediately inside a metallic black octagonal-shaped room. The disturbing thing he did notice, he later recalled, was that it seemed to smell of decaying meat. It was not a nice smell. There were two more of the strange beings inside, so that now he was surrounded by four of them.

A piece of equipment appeared to be scanning his body as he stood with them. He said that the beings communicated with each other in a language he did not know, and their tone was sing-song. They also spoke English though, and one of them enquired how old he was. When he replied that he was in his '70's, the being said he was 'too old and infirm' for their purpose and so they would be letting him leave. He said he then left the craft and walked back to his fishing spot alone.

When he returned home, he told his wife and her friend what had happened to him. They believed him – because they knew him so well and he was not prone to telling fantastical stories, they said, because he had enough of his own true stories to tell about the exciting and dramatic life he'd led, as a soldier and bear hunter, that he didn't need to create stories. Over the years since the encounter, his wife has often been asked whether her now deceased husband ever confessed to making it up as a hoax, but she always insisted he had no need to, he had never read any ufo books, and he had no interest in that sort of thing.

She did however say that he looked shaken when he came home that night, which was very, very unusual for him. Oman Fowler who heads the Surrey Investigation Group on Aerial Phenomena, which boasts among its members pilots, said it was an exciting case which they believed was genuine. When they interviewed him Fowler says, "He came out with things he couldn't possibly have known about unless he'd been studying UFOs for years."

~~~~

In the letters column of French magazine Paris Match came the earliest known abduction survivor report, according to Peter Rogerson of Magonia. (Source: INTCAT files.) A 'Mr GB of Marseille' wrote to tell them of how as a young boy, he had been walking in the Hills close to the Canal Saint-Martin in Paris, when he was seized by two men hiding in the bushes. He said these men were tall, slim and dressed in what appeared to look like metal but flexible diving suits.

The two men then carried him into a large tank-like object which had rectangular portholes. Inside of this there was a couch of some sort, on which the little boy was placed. The 8-year-old boy began to cry as he sat there and a few minutes passed before an opening appeared above him and he suddenly found himself outside and on the ground.

It would seem like he had been taken for only a matter of minutes and yet, when he looked around him he realized he was not where he had originally been and in fact he had to walk for much of the day to get back to where he had been beside the canal.

~~~~

In Strange Magazine of 1994, a Mr. 'P.I.' who lived in Greece had gone to a wooded area close to Lake Volvi, in the Chalkidiki Peninsula in the Thessaloniki region, to cut down some trees. It was August 1938, and he had left before sunrise with his donkey. Almost there, he was passing through an area of thick bushes on either side of the dirt road when he suddenly saw two people standing in a clearing that came into view. As he began to walk closer, he was astonished to see the figures more clearly, and to his shock these two men appeared to be extremely tall, much taller than normal, and their heads were very big. Their eyes, which were watching him, were red. Their faces appeared bloated. They wore clothing that looked like a form of military uniform, but it was not one that he recognized.

Behind them was a large object, the shape of an oval and approximately three feet in height. It was wide enough just to fit the two 'men' inside it, and there was a ladder leading up to an entrance. On seeing this Greek labororer with his donkey, the two 'men' appeared as startled as him and they retreated back up the ladder, closing the man-hole behind them! The farmer quickly left the clearing, baffled and very frightened by these unknown visitors.

~~~~

In July 1951, pilot Fred Reagan was flying his Piper Club small aircraft over Georgia when he claims he felt a mysterious force pull his plane upwards, resulting in it crashing into an 'unidentified flying object. He was hastily taken aboard the craft he says, by 'hovering creatures,' who apparently apologized to him for the air collision, gave him a medical examination, and then pronounced that they had taken away his cancer, which he was actually unaware he had.

He was discovered lying in a field, unconscious yet with not even a scratch on him from his fall from the sky of several thousand feet. His wrecked aircraft was found not far from him. It had nose-dived into the field and was now lying half buried in the ground.

It would seem that although he was cured of his cancer by these 'hovering creatures' aboard their craft, he did in fact later die of a brain tumour, just a couple of years after this encounter. He described these hovering creatures as being approximately 3 feet tall and appearing to look just like metallic 'asparagus stalks!'

~~~~

Less than a month after the famous Kenneth Arnold aerial phenomenon incident close to Mount Ranier, over in San Paolo, Brazil, a survey worker called Jose Higgins along with several of his co-workers, saw a large metallic disc come from the sky and settle on the ground on curved legs. Higgins co-workers all fled but something made Higgins stand his ground and soon he found himself face to face with three 7 ft tall Beings, all wearing transparent overalls with metal boxes on their backs. One entity pointed a tube at him and moved toward him as though to apprehend him. Higgins dodged the entity's attempts and noticed that the entity did not want to follow him into the sunlight.

The entities had large bald heads, big round eyes, no eyebrows or beards, and long legs, he said. They leapt and seemed to be 'frolicking, picking up huge boulders and throwing them around.' The creatures also made holes in the ground, and some later theories were that it could have been their attempt to point out the positions of planets around the sun and pointing particularly to the seventh hole from the centre of their arrangement, which could perhaps be interpreted then as Uranus.

After this, the creatures made their way back to the

craft, and as they re-entered it, it began to make a whistling sound. Higgins account of what he had seen made it into the Brazilian Newspapers. Three weeks after this, this time in Italy, a Professor Johannis was on a walk in the mountains in Carni, north-eastern Italy. Suddenly, he spotted a red metallic disc in a rocky cleft. Then, just as suddenly, he saw that two dwarf-like creatures were now standing behind him, following him. They were moving with tiny steps, their hands perfectly still at their sides and their heads too appeared not to move at all.

As they closed in on him, the professor felt himself become paralysed. The tiny creatures, which he said were less than 3 ft tall, were wearing translucent blue overalls with red collars and red belts. The professor could see no hair, and he described their facial skin as an earthly green color. Their noses were straight, he said, and they had slits for mouths. Their eyes, he said, were large and round and their eyes were protruding.

The professor, on impulse, raised his ice-pick whereupon one of the little creatures placed a hand on its belt and from this belt emerged a puff of smoke and the professor's ice-pick flew from his hand. The professor fell over onto his back.

One of the entities walked forward and seized the professor's ice-pick, and then the creatures made their way back to their craft and re-entered it. Their craft shot up into the ait, hovered over the prone professor, and then seemed to suddenly vanish.

~~~~

From Ted Blocher's HUMCAT Index comes the case of a Mr and Mrs Hector Davis, who were asleep in their camper on the night of 25th August 1968, near Townsville, Queensland, Australia. Suddenly Mr. Davis woke, with a feeling of "suspicion." Looking out the window of the camper, he saw a small being about 4 ½ feet tall sitting in the tree approximately 6 feet off the ground. The being had long blond hair and dazzlingly bright blue eyes, and 'he' was wearing a one-piece suit of grey with matching gloves and shoes, and yet the suit appeared to be corrugated. He wore a kind of cap with an antenna, from which came a faint glow.

Mr. Davis jumped up, intending to go outside and take a closer look at the strange fellow sitting in the tree staring at him but just as he got up, the figure floated from the tree, according to Mr. Davis, as though it felt "guilty it had been caught watching them sleep."

The figure then glided across the road which was about forty feet away, and as the figure glided, its legs seemed to sway as if it was walking on the ground and yet it was moving mid-air. It glided away into the distance, until it completely disappeared into the night....

~~~~

At approximately 8. 30 pm on the evening of October 3rd, 1978, Hideichi Amano drove up a mountain pass outside of Sayama City with his two-year-old daughter. He wanted to use his Ham radio and this area was the best place to pick up a clear radio signal to reach his brother, who lived in another part of the country.

When he reached a suitable location, high enough up on the mountain, he managed to contact his brother with the radio and he spoke to him for several minutes and then after they had ended their conversation, he was about to drive back down the mountain when suddenly the interior of the car became extremely bright.

The light outside of the car was many times brighter than the normal interior lights of the car and yet it shed no light outside of the car, only inside, despite its brightness. He turned to check on his young daughter in the backseat, who to his shock and alarm was now lying across the back seat and frothing at the mouth. He didn't have time to react to do something to help her because at the same time, he became aware of a patch of orange light being beamed through the windscreen onto his stomach. He saw that the light was coming from somewhere in the sky. Then his fear turned to terror when he sensed something metallic being pressed against his temple.

Moving his eyes sideways, he saw an unearthly creature

of humanoid shape standing next to him with a pipe-like device in its mouth and it was this pipe that was being pressed against his temple. From this pipe came an incessant and deafening sound of babbling, as if a record was being played at several times its normal speed. The humanoid being standing next to him had a round face but no neck, two very pointed ears, motionless small eyes that glowed blue-white and a triangular depression in its forehead. Its mouth was clamped shut against the pipe. It had no nose. As the 'music' was piped into his head, Amano said his mind became 'blank.'

After what he estimated to be about 5 minutes, the humanoid then began to fade and slowly vanished. The orange light disappeared and the interior of the car stopped glowing with intense white light. Still terrified and totally confused, Amano managed to start the car and drive off, forgetting at first the condition of his daughter and it was only after he had driven for some minutes did he remember his daughter. He stopped and tended to her and he managed to get her to drink some water, and she make a quick recovery now. He drove straight to the nearest police station to report the baffling, horrifying and terrifying experience but the policemen only laughed at him. Several Japanese UFO investigators however, after listening to the man, became convinced that it was 'the strangest event to have ever happened in Japan."

~~~~

In 1966, 6-year-old Thomas Reed was in his bedroom on the family horse farm in the Berkshires when strange lights began to shine through his bedroom window, and in the hallway outside his bedroom, strange figures appeared in the hallway. The next thing he knew he was in the woods near the farm, then he is inside a craft, where he sees his brother Matthew. He is shown a projection of a large willow tree.

A year passes until another incident occurs. Strange lights begin shining in the windows again and the sound of doors slamming loudly, then he is once more sitting inside a craft with his brother. The next thing he remembers is standing in his driveway and feeling his mother's arms as she scoops him up. She has just got off a horse, having been frantically searching for her sons on horseback.

Fast forward to 18 months later, and the family are driving along Route 7 when they see strange lights in the sky. The car stalls and comes to a stop and he, his brother, grandmother, and mother all find themselves inside a huge room where two odd ant-like figures place them in a cage.

Their next memory is of being back by their car. Despite Tomas Reed suffering years of ridicule and disbelief, the Great Barrington Historical Society & Museum decided to include his very unsettling experiences in their collection, offering it a form of validity. Thomas Reed had also taken a lie-detector test – and passed.

Debbie Opperman, the director of the historical society, told Boston Globe in 2015, "It means we believe it's true. Based on the evidence, and we've given it a lot of thought, we believe this is a true and significant event." Three board members were against the decision - but were in the minority, and although the director says she knows the museum will face backlash for standing by a story that sounds like it comes from a science-fiction book, she is resolute. The museum sits just a couple of miles from where the encounters took place. The museum says that at the time of the encounters, dozens of people in the area also reported seeing strange sights in the sky above them – usually a disc shaped object that was performing incredible manoeuvres. Many of these witnesses called their local radio station.

Reed, who is now 55, said, "We know what we saw, and it was not local. It was definitely off-world. And it affected my whole family, and there has been a lot of post-traumatic stress." He got bullied and beat-up for many years, and his mother, who owned a restaurant in town, had people come in just to take the mickey out of her and her family.

After their third encounter, his mother sold their house as fast as she could, and they moved a few miles away. "This has tarnished our life. This has smeared our family's name. It can only hurt you when someone

Googles your name," he says. Reed has gone on record however to state that some of the newspaper reports have made the details more sensationalist and cliché'd than he would have wished. Of the car incident, he tells MassLive, they were driving over the Sheffield Bridge when they noticed a bright, floating object near their car. Reed describes feeling a sensation like there was a change in pressure, or an electromagnetic field; a dead silence fell over them as the light grew brighter, and they found themselves somewhere else.

"We do remember being in what looked like an airplane hanger. We didn't stay in the car. We were removed from the vehicle, that's true. Where we were, I don't know." He also comments; "FYI, what took place in the area was certainly not isolated to us."

What could his description of it looking like an aircraft hanger tell us about his experience? Was it "off-planet" as he says, or something organised very much on this earth? After all, at the beginning of his account he says, "Strange figures appeared in the hallway. The next thing we knew we were in the woods." He and his brother find themselves inside a 'craft' and he is shown 'a projection of a large willow tree.'

Who were the figures and were they off-planet or human? Why use a projection of a tree? But if it were a human-led incident, what were the 'two odd ant-like figures who 'placed them in a cage....'

Chapter Six

The Missing Hunter

Calling to mind the earlier testimony from the alleged 'black ops' man Aaron McCollum, and his claims of ET-led snatch and grab teams, as well as the strange encounters just described above, Sweet Grass County Sheriff's Lieutenant Alan Ronneberg said, of the search for missing hunter Aaron Hedges, "We just don't have the answer yet. Everything from he got turned around off the trail, got caught in the storm, passed away from hypothermia, to UFOs got him."

Calling it 'A riddle that may never be solved,' Sheriff's Lieutenant Alan Ronneberg, who was involved in the original 12-day search for missing hunter Aaron Hedges, says, "All the interviews have been done, and there are no new leads. All of the theories that have been thought up and been pursued. There is literally a full list - a legal page - of theories out there."

Corporal Gregg Todd, who heads up Park County's Search and Rescue, also said he was unable to draw any firm conclusions. "It's the million-dollar mystery we have right now. We just have so many unanswered questions that it really just doesn't give us much of a direction."

Then, almost a year later, the missing hunter's body was found – in a location that was baffling to all involved. 38-year-old Aaron Hedges had set out with two friends, Greg Leitner of Idaho and Joe Depew of Bozeman to go hunting in the Crazies Mountains of Montana on September 7th, 2014. They set out from Cottonwood Lake Trailhead. His two friends had their rifles, but Aaron preferred to hunt by bow and arrow instead. The last time Aaron was heard from, he had radioed his two friends on his walkie-talkie to tell them he'd missed the turn-off back to camp. He'd been hunting separately from them, as was his practice with his bow and arrow.

Earlier in the day, when they'd all been together, the horse carrying their equipment and provisions had bucked, sending Aaron's sleeping bag flying and rendering it irretrievable. After this, his plan had been to head to the old camp they'd set up the previous year near Sunlight Lake, and he would collect an old sleeping bag there, and then return to his friends at their camp. Aaron never made it back to camp. His friends never saw him again.

It was two days before he was reported missing. There was no cell phone coverage where the two friends were, and they said they'd searched for him themselves. It was his wife who called the police, four days later, when she discovered he was missing. While aspersion could perhaps be cast on his friends, the police, once they became involved in searching for Aaron, ruled them out as having any involvement in his disappearance.

His friends hadn't been overly concerned when he hadn't shown up at their camp – after all, they knew him as an experienced hunter. As soon as searchers arrived to start looking for him, bad weather set in, and soon there was 2 feet of snow. The weather made searching overhead by air practically impossible, and horse-back searchers struggled with visibility and inhospitable terrain. The search was focussed on the Cottonwood Lake Trail with teams of dogs and search and rescue ground crews, along with the National Guard. Night-vision was used and spotlights.

Near Trespass Creek, a search crew came across a wood pile and fire starters, a Camelback bladder with the thin tube removed – leading searchers to think that the person had attempted to locate a fresh water source to drink from, and a pair of boots – which were identified as Aaron's. There was 2 feet of snow on the ground. Why would he remove his boots?

If hypothermia had set in, Aaron may have succumbed to the syndrome of paradoxical undressing, where the body becomes so cold but the person begins to feel extremely hot, and as the cold addles the brain and confusion sets in, the person can find themselves rushing to strip off their clothes, thinking they are boiling hot. If this had been the case for Aaron, then where was he now? How could he possibly have walked very far without his boots, in 2 feet of snow? He would surely have died from hypothermia close-by and easily have been found sadly dead; His body should have been found be nearby, surely? Unless he had another pair of boots with him, and yet, as will be revealed later, this does not seem to have been the case – there is no suggestion that he had any alternative footwear to change into when he took off his boots. The searchers found it very strange that they did not find a body close-by as they continued to search the area.

11 months later, on August 6th, 2015, a butcher from Wyoming called Roger Beslanowitch was waiting for his son-in-law to finish a job fixing a fence at the Rein Anchor Ranch in Sweet Grass County and while waiting he had wandered off to check out the stunning scenery on a ridge. Cutting back through a tree-culling area, he noticed something bright orange on the ground and as he got closer, he saw that it was a hunting vest. Beside it, he found a backpack and some clothes, a bow, and granola wrappers. "My first thought when I saw the clothes piled up against a tree, I just knew there was going to be a body," said Beslanowitch.

The backpack was sitting against a tree, the clothes against another, according to the Powell Tribune. "There's bear activity – where they flip over the rocks to eat the bugs underneath and I just knew there was going to be a body there – but there wasn't," Beslanowitch said.

There was a "vest, socks, shirts and sweatpants." The backpack had holes in it where predators had eaten into it and so it was assumed that the wrappers from the granola bars had also been ferreted by the animals. "I gathered it all up. When I was just about done, I saw a piece of paper and it was a partial license and it had his name on it." The man returned to the ranch owned by his daughter and son-in-law, and he called police.

Aaron Hedges partial skeletal remains were soon located within a small radius of where his vest and backpack had been found. His skeleton had been spread due to "scavenging – everything from weather, ants to bears," said Deputy Sheriff Allan Ronneberg. "Are we able to tell what the man died of? – Probably not," said Sweet Grass County Sheriff Dan Tronrud.

"There's no bullet holes. The pathologist will look to see if there's knife wounds on the bones or hatchet marks but I'm guessing it's going to go down as one of those mysteries".

If he had made it that far, the tragic thing is, the ranch was in eye-shot – he could have seen it from where he was found; "He could see the house," said owner Rebecca Rein. But how had he got there in the first place? 'Search efforts for Aaron Hedges last fall had been carried out on the Livingston side of the mountain, and Beslanowitch's discovery was on the opposite side,' writes the Newspaper, and this is where the mystery truly lies; Aaron Hedges had shed his boots near Trespass Creek. It's quite possible hypothermia was setting in, but how could he have got to where he was found; an estimated 14 to 15 miles (as the crow flies), without boots, in a storm and 2 feet of snow? The area where his skeletal remains were found was on the other side of the mountain.

"It's a totally different area than where we were looking," said Sweet Grass County Sheriff Dan Tronrud.

He put the estimate at least four miles away from where Hedges had been reported missing. Tronrud said Hedges went into the mountains on the Park County side and must have come out on the Sweet Grass County side. "That's a lot of distance to cover."

When Aaron had disappeared, Park County Sheriff Scott Hamilton had said "By the time we were notified, the weather had hit. We're dealing with two feet of snow and it was snowing hard. We deployed a horse team – they made it as far as they could – maybe even further than they should have and came back out. It was tough – very cold. It was snowing hard." Sweet Grass County Deputy Sheriff Alan Ronnenberg said, "It was big heavy flakes. It was really coming down."

According to Billing Gazette, 'Hedges' remains were found about 15 miles from where he was last seen and about 6 miles from where his boots were found. Officials speculate he must have had another pair of shoes, because the rocks were very sharp where Hedges' boots were found, Ronneberg said. Yet no boots were found where his skeleton, backpack, vest and clothes were found. "I'm guessing it's going to go down as one of those mysteries..." said Sweet Grass County Sheriff Dan Tronrud.

What happened to Aaron Hedges? Why would he shed his boots? Did he set off fast, before the weather set in, barefoot; or did something else transport him to the spot where he was found, on the other side of the low mountain, several miles away, barefoot....? How could he possibly have walked so many miles without his boots...?

~~~~

Shaun Ritchi vanished on Halloween night after going out with friends. Since that night, twice his mum has resorted to consulting psychics to try to discover what had happened to her son. She said both psychics told her he was "in the area" as search crews continued to look for him in remote woodland in Strichen, near Fraserburgh in Aberdeenshire Scotland. Extensive searches of the Greenburn area were being combed where he'd last been seen. The area had been repeatedly searched but the only traces found of him were his shoes, his hoodie and his belt.

During the ongoing searches, at the 7 month mark a police helicopter was going back out to search again. His mother was sceptical of any potential success however; "I just want them to find my boy. They told me they're putting the helicopter back out but I don't see why – they say it's because the water levels have dropped in the area they have already searched, but I've been told this for ages."

She had in fact become so desperate for more police action, despite it being the largest search in Scotland's history, that she had been accused and arrested for sending harassing messages to herself and others; playing the pretend role of an imaginary suspect who had taken her son and who was now threatening her and others – she simply couldn't believe foul play wasn't involved and her mind must have become twisted and in such pain that she didn't quite know what she was doing. "I went out to where the clothes were found – and there was a caravan just not far away from there."

The police said, "This has been one of the largest ever search operations carried out by Police Scotland and there is no evidence of any criminality."

He disappeared from remote woodlands near Strichen. He had last been seen on October 31st Halloween night when he and his friends got a ride to a party at a farm in the middle of no-where, according to Scottish Newspapers. At some point he became separated from his friends. He and his friends suddenly began running and split off into two groups, with each group presuming that Shaun had run off with the other group.

A 999 call was sent out near the spot where he went missing, calling for help, but another call was then placed shortly after, cancelling it. Shaun Ritchie's mum Carol-Ann said the call was made from a property close to where her 20-year-old son disappeared. In the first 999 call, a man asked for police to come to a farm in the Greenburn area. But shortly afterwards operators were contacted again and told officers were no longer needed.

Shaun was not reported missing until two days after that night. His friends who had been with him hadn't called the police. A couple of days later, Shaun's shoes, his hoodie and his belt were found in the marshlands near where he was last seen by his friends. It was suggested that he had most likely been suffering from hypothermia and had undressed – a behaviour known as 'paradoxical undressing' and an action that can be very common if a person becomes extremely cold. After getting extremely cold, their body will then begin to feel extremely hot as hypothermia begins to set in and the heat they are feeling can lead them to feel a frantic urge to shed their clothes – the hypothermia stops rational thought from telling them this makes no sense as their brain becomes foggy and confused.

It was hypothesised that as hypothermia set in, Shaun had shed his clothes and then lay down to sleep, another symptom of hypothermia, with him even possibly burrowing in an attempt to try to seek some form of shelter. He had fallen asleep where he lay and had died from the cold, sinking into the bog and never being found. That was the hypothesis of the police, as the fields were marshy and full of bogs.

The bogs had all been searched however, and yet his body had not been found. Thousands of police man-hours had been spent since he vanished after running from something that night, from a remote farmhouse surrounded by boggy fields and thick woodlands.

The police, it seems, could not have involved more experts than they did, in their search for him. Alongside inch by inch searches by huge numbers of personal, in the fields and bogs and woods, covering 21 square kilometres in what police called 'challenging terrain,' they also brought in 27 search dogs, RAF Mountain rescue, divers, ground-penetrating radar, criminal psychological profilers, geo-scientists, and soil experts.

They consulted forensic scientists Professor Lorna Dawson, head of Social Science, and Dr. Alastair Ruffell, a forensic geoscientist, who studied soil samples and vegetation found on his hoodie belt and shoes, to try to identify places he had been in. "At the James Hutton Institute, we work with police and investigators to compare traces of such material on objects or clothing to inform police in developing search strategies and prioritising areas of search, based on where someone might have stood or walked," said Professor Dawson.

His father, Charlie Reid said he believed, "He has definitely not walked out of there. Someone has taken him out of that area and he has been murdered." His father said that the last time his son had been seen, he'd been with a group who had travelled in a van to a remote farmhouse for a party. "Something happened that led them to run and they split into two groups. Each group thought he was with the other group. They all got home that night – except him."

It was a freezing night when he disappeared, with temperatures going below zero. "There's no way Shaun walked out of the area where his shoes were found. He couldn't have..." But no vehicle tyre tracks were found.Mountain rescue teams had used over 20 search dogs. His father had brought in Glasgow K9 search and Recovery Group with its cadaver dog. The dog however failed to find any trace of his son. Police searches had found tiny traces of animal bones, so the search had been very comprehensive, leaving no spot unturned. "The dog going through the peat bogs and trees was exhausted – it's tough going there. Divers have been all through the bogs – there's no way you would get very far without his clothes. People with full body waterproofs and walking sticks struggled." In fact, one of the policemen broke his leg. The police said that while they had not ruled out foul play, there was also no evidence to suggest Shawn had been killed.

Detective Chief Inspector Matt Mackat, leading the investigation during some of the searches said, "We have left absolutely no stone unturned and all I would say Is I will never ignore the prospect of criminality – but I have found no evidence to date to suggest that Shaun has been the victim of any crime. We have no definitive evidential lines that we can follow that suggest he went elsewhere. It is surprising we haven't found Shaun, given that it would be difficult to see how someone could get beyond that area... but we haven't found him."

In other words, they had found no evidence to suggest he had walked or run out of there – the dogs would have tracked him, the searchers would have found his tracks, the dogs would have picked up on his scent, particularly given that they had his hoodie belt and shoes to use at the scene of his disappearance, but they found no trace of him. It was also believed to have been highly unlikely he could have got out of there on his own with no shoes, no warm clothing, no transport. The search police teams found no tyre tracks to indicate he had been transported out of there. Certainly, with detectives and even criminal and psychological profilers used, it has to be assumed that they fully ruled this out through their investigations and extensive enquiries, although they have not released their findings to the public; it hasn't been revealed who was at the farmhouse that night, nor why the 999 call was made and then cancelled. "There is no evidence to date that Shaun has been the victim of a crime," said Inspector Mackay.

Martin Little for Scotland's PressandJournal, retraced the young man's steps. 'Underfoot was wet and muddy, whilst rocks and an uneven road meant you had to watch your step. The walk was difficult enough in May. It didn't bear thinking what it would be like on a freezing, stormy November night. I could see the helplessness of his situation. Dark, freezing and miles from home, in one of the north-east's most unforgiving landscapes. We carried along the road until we came to the bog where police divers had spent days searching. It was now alive with frogs and insects. Hopping over the fence we ventured into the woodland behind it. Walking was hard going, you sank further into the saturated ground with each step. We didn't last long before heading back. For Shaun, getting home without help in those conditions would have been an impossible task.'

Carol-Ann, 37, said the circumstances of her son's disappearance were "a mystery". All that was left of him was his shoes, hoodie and belt, recovered from the marshland near where he was last seen. "There's no way Shaun walked out of the area where his shoes were found. He couldn't have..." says his father. Then where is he? Why has he not been found there, in the marshlands and woodland? What happened that night... and where is he....? No shoes, no tyre tracks, no scent, no body....

Chapter Seven

In the Sky & Underground

Again, calling to mind the words of alleged whistle-blower Aaron McCollum and the possible existence of underground bases and snatch teams, on 10th September 2016, the Huddersfield Examiner asked, "Is there an Underground UFO base at Scammonden Dam Reservoir?" The article detailed the latest sighting. 'A mother and daughter were left terrified after spotting a UFO in the Sky above the M62 near the dam.' The Dam is the only reservoir in England with a motorway going over it. Scammonden Dam carries the motorway over Deanhead Valley in the Pennines. It was a difficult engineering project when it was built, due to the proximity of peat bogs. Excavation for the dam and reservoir began in 1963 and required the removal of 713,000 cubic metres of peat bog in order to reach the solid rock base 13 metres below ground level.

It's situated in the Pennines, a range of mountains and hills separating North West England and North East England. It's sometimes called 'the Backbone of England.' The Pennine Hills form an almost continuous range of hills stretching northwards from the Peak District. The reservoir is 1.4 km in length. The landscape around it is comprised of woodland and rough pastures and moorland.

The mother and daughter who were 'left terrified after spotting a UFO in the Sky above the M62 near the dam' told the Huddersfield Daily Examiner; "It was a clear night, and on the moors there were no road lights. It was completely pitch dark. Suddenly as I am driving on the road, to my left a very bright light appeared over the moor above us. It was disc-shaped, with a green and red light. It was slowly moving across the road high above our car. My daughter also noticed two blue lights as well, on the rim of the object. The craft also spun slowly. We were in absolute shock. I kept driving and it made its way across the valley. As we watched, in a blink of an eye it totally vanished. We literally were terrified and were panicking."

The Huddersfield Examiner says, that on a different occasion 'Another person reported seeing an object floating over the dam for 10 minutes before descending down inside it. Several people have claimed to see flying triangles silently hovering in the sky, before flying off at speeds far beyond any kind of military jet.' It continues; 'A couple were driving along the country road next to the dam when they saw a triangular craft enter the dam, then a classic saucer-shape craft exits the dam. Moments later a mist formed out of nowhere and the next thing they knew they were driving in the wrong direction on the road running parallel to the road they were originally on. Over the following months, they came to believe they had been abducted.'

Mark Gibbons, former director of investigations for British Earth and Aerial Mysteries Society and writer in UFO magazine, claims to have been with the couple on another occasion, and he says an object, a hovering triangle, was motionless and quiet in the sky. "We observed it for 20 minutes then decided to leave. The craft began to follow us. We speeded up and the craft also speeded up. It was a clear night, then out of no-where a large cloud appeared and the craft entered it. The cloud then seemed to disappear, and the craft with it. In my mind there is something going on up at Scammonden."

"The couple were left shaken and they didn't know what happened. Over the months, more memories came back and the abduction picture began to form, but it was what they claimed that they saw at the dam which interested me." Mr Gibbons said a few years later his files on UFO activity at Scammonden, including a letter from RAF Fylingdales in North Yorkshire, were mysteriously stolen. He added: "In my mind, I am sure there is something going on up at Scammonden, be it alien or military. I am sure that there is an underground base at the dam, as it is the only dam in the country with a steel reinforced base under the concrete base."

Two weeks after the mother and daughter car incident at Scammendon moor, 'A small, bright green triangle was seen hovering over Bolster Moor at 10.33pm.' The sighting was reported on the website uk-ufo.co.uk by James D, who said: "Noticed a bright green small triangle over Bolster Moor looking from Linthwaite. Approximately five seconds later it went at high speed away from Bolster Moor in the direction of Scapegoat Hill. It then disappeared from view."

On November 30th, a man called Tom Lawton reported seeing a 'shimmering light' flying over Emley Moor Mast, fifteen minutes away from the Reservoir. It was there for approximately 30 minutes, before it rose slowly up into the sky, and disappeared, after being visible for two hours.

A report submitted to BEAMS on December 3rd, 2016, was of a 'Triangle UFO Seen Bradford Moor, heading towards Scammonden Dam.' In a UFOINFO Sighting Report, on 16th December 2006, at 6pm, a witness reported a 'Circle/sphere emitting very bright white/yellow light when visible. Became invisible but reappeared 2 seconds later in a 2nd location. The sighting took place 'between Scapegoat Hill and Scammonden Reservoir.' The witness said, "We were returning from a football match, driving along A62, coming down from Standedge top towards Marsden, when we became aware of what looked like a sunset in highly illuminated dense clouds. The position ruled out the presence of the sun as it had already been dark for two hours. For a second, it seemed to shine with what was almost a beam over a particular area of Scapegoat Hill. Then the light went out. I looked around and within seconds noticed a highly illuminated area of dense cloud in a different place - Scammonden Reservoir. We lost sight of this after a few seconds." The height and distance, according to the witness was an estimated "height of 500 feet, 2 miles away." And it was 'Static.'

In October 2008, The Wakefield Express wrote; 'Secret X-files reveal UFO sightings in Wakefield district. Unexplained reports of a strange 200-foot object hovering in the skies have emerged after secret government files were released.' Again, it was at Emley Moor, fifteen minutes away from the Scammendon Reservoir. 'Mystery still surrounds the sightings of a huge cylinder-shaped craft which stunned eyewitnesses at Emley Moor in the early hours of November 2, 1986.'

'Police officers received reports of two bright lights in the sky above Emley mast at around 4am, according to unveiled Ministry of Defence documents.' Officers arrived on the scene at around 4.20am and watched the UFO, which was around 1,200 feet above the mast and had bright white lights at either end. An unnamed police officer who attended the scene said: "On first seeing the object, it was totally static, not moving in any direction. It appeared to be hovering." The other unnamed police officer who attended said in the government report: "It did not move in any direction, though it appeared to wobble and distort." Nine different witnesses reported seeing the object in the sky, and they said that it appeared to change colour from red to green before it then flew off in an eastwards direction. The police officers reported the sighting to the Civil Aviation Authority, however they could offer no answer, although they confirmed that it was not a commercial or private aircraft in the sky.

One report from November 2016 cites; 'I have seen over Bradford Moor, about the same time, usually on a Tuesday and a Wednesday night, a set of triangle lights with a red light in centre. Silent and completely different to aircraft lights. It comes or heads towards the same direction, which when I looked on Google Earth, would have taken it towards a place called Scammonden Dam. I work as a security guard. One morning about 7.10 am I saw a triangle craft fly over the site at work. It was a grey-blue colour about the size of a F117 (Nighthawk) aircraft. It was heading in the same direction as the other lights I have seen.'

In 1986, John Stoddard and his wife were staying in a cottage on Bonsall Moor in the Derbyshire Dales. On this particular night, they were due to leave and drive home, having spent the Christmas Holidays there. It was just gone 7. 20 pm when Mr. Stoddard stood outside and glanced up into the sky. He noticed that one of the Stars was moving – in the direction of where he was standing, coming from over the hills in the distance. By the time his wife had come out and joined him, the 'Star' was now flying up to him at a low speed of, he guessed, 10 miles an hour. It was now just over the trees in the adjacent field. His wife watched it too and it suddenly opened up into a giant triangle with white lights all around it. They estimated it to be about the size of a double-decker bus. They described feeling "excited" but also very scared by what they saw. The object then moved very slowly out of view, going over the Moors.

Witness Sue Sill, from the village of Outlane near Huddersfield, and just 3 miles from Scammendon Reservoir, says she was abducted in 2010, at the same time that mysterious crop circles appeared nearby, and she says she has been having strange experiences ever since, recurring usually every few weeks. She claims to have filmed UFOs all around the area, including Scammonden Reservoir. She said, "In July 2010, a crop circle had appeared at Castle Hill." Castle Hill is a hill-top with an ancient monument, 8 miles from the reservoir and dam. She said; "I was sorting my things out for the morning and running a bath. I walked back into the bedroom and it was like I had gone into a trance. I sat down on the bed and the next thing I knew, some figures appeared. They were small, and they had black skin or were wearing black suits. They had long, thin arms and their faces were obscured, like a liquid. I was thinking, 'Oh my God, what's happening?'

"They came to the side of the bed and something like a veil came over me. The next thing I knew I was in a craft looking at Earth. The craft was iridescent like a bubble, I could see everything around me. I was thinking, 'How can I be looking at the Earth?' The creatures spoke with telepathy and were showing me Earth. At once, there was a massive explosion on Earth, like a mushroom, and my heart sunk. One of the creatures put its hand on my shoulder. It was a long middle finger. It was like it was feeding off my emotions. I remember the creature saying, 'Don't worry, you will be alright'.

Then, all of a sudden, she woke up and found herself lying fully dressed lying on her bed. Hours had passed since her last memories of being in her bedroom and running the bath. "I tried to get up, but I couldn't stand. I felt sick. I tried to do my normal routine, getting ready for work, but it was like I was jetlagged. I saw my neighbour and he asked me what was wrong. I said, "I think I've been abducted". He just laughed. I thought I was going crazy, so I went to the doctor. He just looked at me and sent me straight to a psychiatrist, who said I was okay."

Since that day, she says she has regularly seen UFO's or had other unexplainable experiences every few weeks, and incredibly, these anomalous incidents often occur when in the presence of her family. "If I'm having delusions, the people who are with me are having them too," she says. She has shared many photos taken at family get-togethers, where strange objects appear to loom in the sky close-by, such as the photo at her granddaughter's birthday party where a pear-shaped 'UFO' appears. She says she knows people are sceptical of course. "These craft have been visiting my property since summer of 2015. I have photos (day and night ones). I have no idea what they are, but they most certainly are not imagined. There has also been poltergeist-type activity in the home, that started when these "things" began showing up."

But could her experiences perhaps have been a MILAB experience, MILAB being a military abduction by black ops on behalf of a secret government agency, rather than an alien one? Given that her description of the "things" were dressed in black – they had "black skin or were wearing black suits. They had long, thin arms and their faces were obscured."

On 17th February 2010, this next witness says; 'I drove my dog to Temple Newsam, just south of Halton Moor. Temple Newsam is a Tudor/Jacobean House and vast grounds. It's referred to as 'Neuhusam' in the Doomsday Book and was given to the Knights Templar in 1155. It was here that a Knights Templar Preceptory, a local chapter, was set up.

'At approximately 11 p.m. I let the dog out of the car and she ran off. My dog is not the best behaved at all times, but she had disappeared. I stood for about 20 minutes shouting for her. While I stood in the dark, I was aware of a brightness above me, but I didn't look up immediately, as I was angry with the dog. As I looked into the darkness for my dog, I saw an oval shaped light in the field, passing through low floss-type cloud. I estimate the object to be approximately 1000 meters away. There was no noise at all. Hard to estimate the size of the light but at a guess size, 4 double decker buses. A relative saw the object from a different location on the same night. I don't believe in E.T.'s but I did see a UFO. Three nights after this sighting I saw the same light again about 2 miles from the first location. This time the light was bigger in size but still using cloud for cover. It was moving much faster.'

Interestingly, another report from November 15th 2010, also involves Temple Newsam. 'Myself and my wife were travelling on the A1 from Colton to Rothwell. As we travelled adjacent to Temple Newsam, we witnessed a large glowing white-blue object traveling directly above us at great speed. The object was too big to be a shooting star and far too fast to be a plane or helicopter. I do not recall it having jet stream. It's possibly the weirdest thing I have seen. At the time, myself and my wife both looked at each other and said: 'What the hell was that?'

From all the reports of sightings of unidentified lights or crafts in the sky near to, heading to, or leaving Scammendon Reservoir, is there really something very mysterious going on at the Reservoir? Could there really be a secret underground base hidden below? Well, in a curious forum on the website http://www.whale.to/b , it would seem that the Newspaper report from 2016, asking, "Is there an Underground UFO base at Scammonden Dam?" was ten years late to the party. The thread in the forum of this website was started on June 7th, 2006, and it was discussing an alleged 'Underground Base' at Scammendon Reservoir.

In this discussion, it had gone way beyond the speculation and theory of an Underground Alien Base being there. Instead, it was discussing ways to shut it down and put it out of action. How they knew there was an Alien Base is not exactly explained, although it would appear that those involved in the discussion were only a few in number and appeared to have garnered the ability to dowse and do etheric battle.

To dowse, or dowsing is a type of divination used to locate items in the ground or under the ground, such as streams, oil, and precious metals. It employs the use of dowsing rods rather than scientific or engineering equipment and is more to do with the sensitivity of the user's ability to pick up on energies within the earth, which will move the divining rod in one direction or another, indicating to the dowser that they have hit on their target. Although it cannot be taught necessarily, and is most usually seen as pseudoscience, it can also be incredibly accurate.

Having said that it's not recognised scientifically, actually in 2017 the UK's Guardian Broadsheet newspaper reported, 'Ten of the 12 water companies in the UK have admitted they are still using the practice of water dowsing, and dowsers, or 'water witchers.' Water companies did and had for many years been employing the use of dowsing to locate broken water pipes. 'Some water companies insisted the practice could be as effective than modern methods,' The Guardian reported. In fact, when asked, Severn Trent Water replied, 'We've found that some of the older methods are just as effective than the new ones.' Anglican Water agreed.

Back on the small forum of water dowsers and etheric warriors discussing how to combat the Alien base under Scammendon reservoir, a man called Don Croft began by telling the others that they were under attack by hackers. 'Struck a nerve. One confirmation is unable to post due to hacker interference. I'm getting similar interference right now.' He advises those who intend to visit the reservoir on how to investigate it for the alien presence; 'Take note of changes in the atmosphere, ambience, plant and animal life. The physical and other sensory confirmations are what build our confidence and lend substance and credence and empirical evidence.'

Then he issues what would be a threat if an Alien race were there, in a base under the water. 'Any parasitic alien who tried to abduct a gifter would literally get blasted by orgone - because we become orgone capacitors from doing this work - Pure life force - and that can be fatal to parasites and predators, and they seem to know that. The stupider and more arrogant ones among the sewer rat hierarchies (he means the underground Aliens, and this seems to imply he is saying he has encountered if not indeed battled with them) don't respect this truth and they get stung.'

He then describes how to 'take out' an alien base, in the manner in which, it would seem, this small group, whoever they actually are, believe they have done before. Don Croft himself is an 'etheric warrior,' who utilizes Orgone to destroy the Bases. He does this through 'Earth Pipes.' 'Fill a toilet paper core tube with orgonite and a single 1" long quartz crystal of any quality, wrap in a coil, and drop it down a fencepost or sign pole that's set in the ground. You can get a stronger effect by pounding in three earthpipes together in a triangle formation to disrupt and neutralize underground predatory tech and disabling underground sources of deadly energy.'

'Earthpipes have a lot of throw. If a base can't be surrounded, it's pretty easy to take it out by putting groups of earthpipes on opposite sides, as close to the property as possible. It's not necessary to risk being shot by the sewer rats mercenaries (he means Aliens) to take out an underground base. Water gifts have a lot more throw than on land. If you're dowsing, you might find it easier to determine how many earthpipes are needed to drive the rats (he means Aliens) from their underground bases. I'm dowsing seventeen in this case, which indicates either a very large underground base, a particularly heinous one, or both.'

He continues, in deadly seriousness, 'It took that many earthpipes for us to do the huge, ancient base under Death Valley. The threat represented by these horrible underground facilities is quite severe, in my opinion, and very widespread. The underground bases are high priority, taking back the earth grid and neutralizing satanic institutions and killing sites.' He adds, 'Most of the cell towers are on the earth grid and vortices, and most of the satanic sites are also on or close to these features.'

A man called 'Christian' on the forum, claims he has already surreptitiously visited the dam, for the purposes of sabotaging and destroying the alleged underground base. 'Made my first foray this week. There's two transmitters - HAARP? The fenced area around it contains a few small buildings, and what appears to be air vents sticking out of the ground. There are reports going back over 30 years, of people entering one of these buildings and not coming back out.'

'I buried two EP's (Earth Pipes) just outside the perimeter fence and tossed 5 TB's over the fence into the scrubs. The Dam isn't easy to get around. The rest of the shore seemed quite steep and will require a long walk down from the ridge. I hammered one EP (Earth pipe) in at the thin end of Scammonden water,' chillingly, he says, 'Near where an abduction experience has been reported, and tossed a TB in the brook. I will be going back up there again to finish the job soon. I've no idea how many should be sufficient for a base, but I felt a desire to saturate the place with orgonite. Maybe several trips required. Wore my harmonic protector the whole time - the abduction story was unsettling!"

~~~~

According to L.Savage, The Phoenix Liberator, July, 1992; Val Valerian & Michael Lindemann; William F. Hamilton III; 'Back in 1999, 'Several accounts suggest that the military-industrial complex entered into a collaboration with a parasitical alien race. In exchange for advanced techn, the industrialists allowed the aliens to access the trillion dollar military-industrial underground network, to carry out "genetic experiments".

'Those who received the new 'Trojan horse' techno also received major mind-control programming, and as a result, the underground networks are assimilated by the alien collective, by effectively controlling the minds of those people who pose the greatest threat to alien imperialism; those with the access to the technology."

"There are reportedly cloned humans with cybernetic minds and reptilian DNA who work in these facilities. They are known as 'The Orange,' because of their stalk-like yellowish/ reddish hair, along with Greys, Reptiloids, Military Black Ops, and others. These aliens create a facade of benevolence towards the "programmed" humans who work in the underground facilities. Reports of abductions and dissections of humans abound, reportedly with the purpose of "finding our weaknesses and learning how to control us."

At Tehachapi, (Arizona) there are open silos where hovering basket-ball size drones or 'spy-bees' monitor all activity above and below ground, where "ground-scrapers" descend at least 2 miles and 42 sub-levels, connecting to other facilities via tunnels and to more ancient alien cavern domains.' (both natural and artificial.)

This site is supposedly "located of Little Oak Canyon," NW of Lancaster. "These aliens have been known to abduct or even kill some who have reported their presence there, because the aliens operate inside our government via the Military-Industrial Trojan horse which operates outside of Congress oversight and do not want their subversive activities to be discovered by the masses.

'Just west of Ottawa, is allegedly the location of an "alien projects" centre. Huge facilities. An alien 'collective' infiltrated the military/ government complex via sell-out Industrialists, but in making deals, they have succeeded only in being drawn deep into their occult - technological control. The tech and intellect of the aliens, combined with their mastery of sorcery and supernatural warfare has made battle futile except for those who have succeeded in acquiring the supernatural power directly from the Creator - necessary to meet and defeat the aliens in the supernatural realm, and in turn, the collective; which is incarnated and organized by Luciferian entities behind the scenes. In this war, the Chaplain is of equal if not greater value than the general as the aliens attack humankind via technological sorcery.'

'These places are the most deserted places on earth. Many have been known to go to these places and never come back, or if they do, they are NEVER the same....' source: L. Savage.'

One lady says; on 'tall-white-aliens.com' 'I started my hiking at the First Water Trailhead Superstition Wilderness, Arizona with the intention of going to Weaver's Needle. I followed it to a fork just beyond what looks like "Aylors Caballo Camp"? I ran out of water at about that point. I realized I wasn't going to reach Weaver's Needle, so I decided at that point to try to make it back, but I had encountered two rattlesnakes in the same spot further back and they were not happy that I was trying to get past them, so I decided to go a different direction. I turned left onto what looks like "Bull Pass Trail" and followed it a way to Dutchman's

Trail. Then I turned left on Military Trail. It has a lot of ups and downs and really narrow areas with long drops. I lost my footing a few times because of loose rocks. I reached Boulder Trail and grew increasingly weak and dehydrated. I am frankly amazed I got as far as I did before collapsing.

When I was lying exhausted in a dry riverbed, a human figure came to me. She's wearing a long dark robe with a hood. She's reaching for something close to the ground. Her face was like a human, but she had big red-orange eyes with a vertical pupil, and the skin was dark green. The nose on the face was flat and invisible. When she noticed that I was awake and looking at her, I seem to have fallen into darkness - like I was turned off.

I woke up surprised to feel a lot of strength. I didn't know what kind of creature it was, but she saved my life. I followed the path until I came to people where I had help. My friend, who lived in the area, had warned me about hiking those trails, because he said that those trails were where the majority of the bad stuff happened in the area. He told me once that a friend of his had found an entrance to an underground facility and that he himself had investigated it.

Perhaps my salvation was in their purposes, and not out of a desire to help. If I died there, it would lead more people to search for me. They would explore the area and perhaps would have stumbled across the entrance to some underground facilities.

Cossette Willoughby tells of a very strange experience she and her husband Ken had, (source: subterraneanbases.com) while staying in a heavily wooded area about 20 miles from Quincy, California. She claims they saw "An old man" with white hair, who was wearing a white shirt and dark trousers. He "swung his head from side to side like a lizard as he walked. He had a "reptilian appearance," and he was apparently carrying a very decorative cane, with a round ball at the top of it which had a carving of cobras wound around the stick."

Although she is certain "he" was aware of their presence, the "man" ignored them as he walked out of the woods, across the small path and disappeared into the woods again in an area where "there is no sign of civilization for miles around."

Chapter Eight

Dark-Eyed Abductors

Locally known as 'The Devil's Bonfire,' the Longendale Lights have been haunting the barren and lonely stone crags near Bleaklow for many many years, going back to earlier centuries. The 'Devil's Bonfire' is located between greater Manchester and the Peak District National Park, in Derbyshire, England. Longdale means "long wooded valley." It is set in remote, rugged high moorland that spans about ten miles and is overlooked by the peaks of Bleaklow and Shining Clough. A small one lane road runs the perimeter of it, but it can only really be accessed on foot. It's a bleak and wild isolated spot on the moors.

The haunting lights that appear there seem to be focused most on a spot called the 'Devil's Elbow,' and the valley and the surrounding area has a reputation for strange phenomena, including unexplained lights and apparitions.

Matthew Corrigan from the local newspaper, The High Peak & Marple Review says 'By day the Pass is beautiful, its tree-lined hillsides and reservoirs providing a scenic backdrop whatever time of year. But as the sun begins to fall something changes. Perhaps it's the shadows of the peaks looming menacingly overhead. Perhaps it's the loneliness; it's not a good place for the engine to misfire. Or perhaps it's something altogether more primeval, an irrational fear awakened by the otherworldly sense of melancholy that hangs palpably in the air. Early witnesses referred to 'Devil's Bonfires.'

A young woman called Laverne Marshall reportedly had a terrifying encounter with the mysterious Longdendale lights late one night on February 14th, 1995. She was returning to her home in Glossop, after driving her son to the Airport. Her daughter Stacey was accompanying her, and her baby, and they were both in the back seats. The mother and daughter were chatting casually as she drove home, going through the isolated moorland when "all of a sudden, these little really bright light balls appeared on the dash. They were dancing up and down just like they were being controlled by a juggler. The first thing I did was to look up to see if a plane was going over; but there was nothing above us. There were no houses around, and there were no headlights behind me."

"I said to Stacey straight away; "Take that torch off the baby" but she shouted back "Mum, it's not turned on." Stacey grabbed the baby off the back seat and held her and as she did so these lights moved onto the roof of the car." Laverne watched in her rear-view mirror, helpless to do anything as seven to eight tiny, incredibly bright bobbing lights moved around inside their car. She carried on driving, too scared to stop on the dark Moors. There was no refuge, no safety outside of the car. Just moorland. The jiggling lights, the size of golf-balls then split up into two groups. "We sat speechless as they went to the back window and then they each moved back in single file to the dash, where they regrouped, almost as if they were marching in order."

Then abruptly they disappeared. "I don't know where they came from, I don't know where they went, but one minute they were there, the next minute they'd gone!"

The High Peak & Marple Review also relates the case of Lennie Blake who was home one evening in January 2013, in Hollingworth, a few miles away from the moorland, when something caught her eye outside the window. 'Looking towards the moors, she became transfixed by a series of white lights in the sky. Moving as a group they were repeatedly making formations and splitting apart, at one point forming a very obvious line before dropping out of view behind the hillside.'

BBC Radio 4, in 1999 interviewed "Debbie," who is a local. 'Once a month, Debbie hooks up the video camera to the computer and then onto the Internet, allowing people all over the world a chance to glimpse the Longdendale lights. "They are like ephemeral flames that sometimes light up the whole valley," she explains. Jill Armitage of 'Paranormal Derbyshire,' notes that in January 1989, the Charlesworth family reported 'a midnight sighting. They described the light as unmoving and lighting up the valley like a floodlight. It had rays of light coming out and then all of a sudden it was not there anymore. At first, they thought it might be a car headlight but when they later compared this with a car on the hillside, it was nothing like it. The light they had seen was much brighter and about half the size of the full moon.

Former Leader of the Glossop Mountain Rescue Team, Philip Shaw told the High Peak & Marple Review that the team's record of strange lights date back to 1973. He of course is well aware that many of these sightings have a rational and logical explanation – changing weather conditions for example which can alter the vision of the landscape and cause it to become misty or foggy. Some of the sightings defy explanation however – such as Shaw's own sighting in 1980 of a large orange light that he first thought was a searchlight, located on the top of the moor, but, "it was broad daylight and access by vehicle was impossible." Some of his colleague has seen the smaller dancing lights.

The Peak District mountain rescue team has been called

out many times by visitors reporting lights on the moors in the mistaken assumption that walkers are lost in the night. On the night of March 24, 1997, the Mountain Rescue teams received three separate very disturbing calls, all reporting that an aircraft was flying extremely low over the moors and was going to crash. A couple also shortly afterwards called to report hearing the crash, and seeing the sky lit up by an orange glow.

According to reporter Caroline Perry, 'The seven mountain rescue controllers immediately dispatched their teams, in the hopes of dragging survivors from the wreckage. For 15 hours, more than 140 people plus an RAF helicopter searched every inch of the moorlands. Yet no trace was found of any aircraft.' No plane was ever reported missing. One explanation put forward was that the witnesses might have been experiencing a replay of tragic 1948 air crash when a US B29 crashed on a routine flight killing all the crew. 'The mountain rescue teams have been called out endless times to investigate - only to find nothing. This has been going on for over 20 years and reports are so regular that police no longer pass on sightings of mystery lights unless they feel it is a genuine sighting of a red distress flare.'

The strange lights that move and dance near the Devil's Elbow have often been mistaken for hiker's carrying torches, flashlight beams of search parties, distress flares, or ball lightning, but it is known that hikers often become disorientated by the unnatural lights. On seeing the lights, they will often think that they are coming from a village in the distance and they have followed the lights only to find that the lights then mysteriously move further away, almost as though they are luring the hikers onwards to an unknown fate....

~~~~

Harperrig Reservoir lies to the far west of the Pentland Hills Regional Park, a stunning range of hills in the Scottish Borders that stretch from the City of Edinburgh down to the small village of Carlops. It is a mixture of publicly-owned land and private land used for farming and sport shooting. The reservoir lies alongside the A70 road west of Balerno at the foot of the Cauldstane Slap, the pass between West Cairn and East Cairn Hills. There is an old Castle at the Reservoir called Cairns Castle, thought to have built around 1440. It is a ruin keep; a 'keep' being a fortified tower. All that is left of it is a tower and a small square wing. The castle stands on a raised mound jutting out into the Reservoir, which is filled by the water of the river Leith. The reservoir sits to the far west of the Pentland Regional Park. On the East side sits the famous Rosslyn Chapel, as featured in Dan Brown's novel, The Da Vinci Code. The chapel has been the subject of speculative theories concerning a connection with the Knights Templar, the Freemasons and The Holy Grail.

It was at this reservoir nearby that; 'UFO abduction claim sparked secret military probe,' says The Scotsman Newspaper. 'Rather than being dismissed at the time as Hollywood fantasy, the 1992 incident was taken seriously enough to be investigated by the Ministry of Defence.' On August 17th, 1992, 33-year-old ambulance technician Garry Wood from Edinburgh, was driving to Tarbrax, in South Lanarkshire, accompanied by Colin Wright, 25. They were going to deliver a satellite TV to their friend. It was approximately 10 pm. They were driving along the A70 and as they passed Harperrigg Reservoir, suddenly Colin exclaimed; "What the hell is that!" pointing upward into the night sky.

In the sky was a two-tiered disc-shaped black object, approximately 20 feet above the front of their car. It came into view as they rounded a corner. It had been partially hidden by trees. It was shiny, metallic. It had no windows. Garry hit the accelerator pedal in an attempt to accelerate away from the object. In fact, as Colin would later say, Garry drove "like a madman." As they drove underneath the unidentified black object in the sky, a bright light beamed down on them and what happened next is an account of pure horror.

The encounter they had was later revealed in de-classified Ministry of Defence documents, released in 2012. A two-page report on what became known as the "A70 incident" was sent to the Ministry of Defence's UFO desk in 1996. The document had the heading 'Unexplained Aerial Sighting.' The two men said that they experienced a complete black-out of lights as absolute darkness set in and in fact the blackness around them made Garry think he had crashed the car and they were now dead.

They realized however, that the car was still moving, at an alarming speed. What shocked them most however was that they now seemed to be going in the opposite direction, yet they had no memory of having turned the car around. Their seatbelts were also hanging off. They were both trembling violently. The mysterious object above them had disappeared, and they somehow managed to calm down enough to make their way to their destination, the friend's house. When they arrived, it should have been about 40 minutes later, according to the time it usually took them and the distance from where they were, but they were stunned to discover that when their friend called out from his bedroom window angrily asking what the heck they were doing knocking on his door, it was not 10.45 pm, the time they had believed it was, but it was past 1 am instead.

The official classified documents about the incident demonstrates that the Ministry of Defence took the account somewhat seriously, given that they classified the report. It states that Garry was driving "When the object dropped a curtain of white light in front of the car. His friend blacked out for what seemed like 10-15 seconds. He thought he had died. When he woke up, the car was facing the opposite direction, on the wrong side of the road. When he checked his watch, he had lost about one hour." The 'UFO' is described in the reports as 20 feet in height, 30 feet across, and black in colour, with no lights at all. The two men reported the incident to the police, a doctor, a psychologist and a University.

Speaking in 1996, 4 years after the incident, Garry said; "I saw three creatures coming towards my car. I felt intense pain, like an electric shock. Then I was in some room. I saw these things like wee men moving about, doing something to me. Then this six-foot creature approached. It was grey-white in colour with a large head and a long, slender neck, very slim shoulders and waist. Dark eyes. The arms were like ours but there were four very long fingers." "The little ones were about three feet tall and seemed to do all the work, while the big ones did the communication."

The aliens spoke to him. They said: "Sanctuary – we are here already, and we are coming here." Gary said that a red-hot poker object was put into his eye, and he was surrounded by other crying humans. In the days that passed after their incident, both the men were exhausted – they felt completely drained of all energy and yet they found it impossible to sleep; and when they did eventually manage to sleep, both men had the most dreadful nightmares and they would wake with pounding headaches. Their nightmares were extremely graphic, vivid, and disturbing. When Garry, a mechanic, went to the doctor's for help, he was referred to the hospital to have an MRI scan and a spinal tap. Neither procedure found any anomalies or problems. On the advice of the British UFO Association, who they also contacted for help, they underwent hypnotic regression therapy, in an effort to reveal what had really happened to them that night during their period of missing time.

In the first session, Garry found himself bursting into tears. He was unable to be consoled. He and his friend both recalled memories of sitting in the car when three humanoid creatures approached the car and opened the car doors. Garry was taken out of the car by the humanoids and lain on a stretcher, according to Colin. Garry said, "I saw three creatures coming toward the car. I felt intense pain – like an electric shock. Then, I was in a room and I saw these things-like-men moving around, doing something to me. Then a six-foot creature approached me!"

Colin remembered being taken through a corridor that was circular. When he reached the end of the corridor, one of the creatures took him inside a room that had no features inside it. It was a bare room, and the creatures stripped his clothes from him and an examination of him began. Most awful of all is that he recalls being naked standing inside a glass container with his ankles tied together. From his vantage point inside the glass container he could see other men and women, also naked, also standing inside glass containers. The room was hazy, as though some kind of smoke or fog was in it, and he also saw something that seemed to be a scanning device. He believed this device was scanning the humans in the glass containers, including him.

As for Colin, he said that he found himself lying prone on a table, but he could not move, even though he didn't think he was tied to the table. He and Garry both stated that while they were held inside the rooms, they could hear screams of agony coming from the other human captives.

Colin confirmed the same descriptions of small humanoid creatures as well as much taller skinner ones. Both men said that there was one specific tall creature who seemed to be in charge. Garry refers to him as 'The Emperor.' Garry asked him what he wanted here. "Sanctuary" came the reply. Both men wept often during their hypno-regression sessions. Garry also took a lie detector test under the supervision of Professor Susan Greenwood for a BBC television program. He passed the test. Although this does not mean he certainly was abducted, it does mean that what he says happened to him, he believes really did happen, and if he wasn't abducted, what else could explain what he went though?

According to Brian Allan of SPI Strange Phenomena

Investigations, Colin was regressed by therapist Helen Walters. In his regression session he says; "I'm cold. I'm getting carried along. Something's looking back at me in the corridor; Aghhh!! it's ugly! It's ugly and it's lurking in that corridor. It seems ancient. Ugly. It's really badly deformed. It thinks its's trying to manipulate me.... It's away. I can hear a noise behind me. I'm staring at a wee creature. It's not very happy with me. I don't think I was supposed to look behind my chair... It's looking back at me with those black eyes... If I try to do anything they'll come round the corner and stop me... Two of them have got me by the feet and are dragging me toward a small archway.... They're not fussy about hurting me... There's a big alien in front of me doing something or taking something out of my head... shooting pain. My brain fees like it's swollen... like it's going to burst ... I can't handle this...."

~~~~

When Jim Sparks claimed to have been abducted in 1988, he says; "There were twelve large humanoid creatures standing in a circle in which I was a part. The creatures appeared to be at least six feet tall. All of them had their heads turned towards the alien who was standing to my immediate left. The face of this creature was like a hologram of a human face superimposed and glowing over the alien's face. This was done to disguise his true appearance.

The Being communicated telepathically and it was out of sync with its lips. As this was going on, it started to rain. The creatures didn't try to get out from under it. They didn't have to: we weren't getting wet. Then they said: "It's time to go."

'Wait, ... I want to see what you look like.'
I'll never forget their response as long as I live:
"It will strike fear in your heart."

'Spinning light began to radiate over their faces and upper bodies. I could see they were huge. Their upper torso was strong, with huge shoulders and a thick, strong neck like football linebackers.'

'You have scales!' Their faces looked like a cross

between a lizard and a snake - nothing at all like the little grey guys. Their eyes were diamond shaped, their pupils were red. Their skulls looked like their brains stuck out over their foreheads, covered by skin.'

~~~~

In another incident, British UFO investigator Margaret Fry reported on a series of events in Wales in 1997. It involved a case of alien abduction, missing time and Men in Black. The events of November 10th, 1997 centred around a family who were driving along on the Bodfair - Landernog road in the mountainous region in North Wales, when all of a sudden their car was engulfed by a purple craft that seemed to attach itself to their car. The next memory any of the family in the car had was that the craft had just disappeared into thin air. Terror and horror gripped them all in those brief moments, first as the craft appeared and second as they regained their next sensations and realized it was gone.

They were still driving along the highway, but now they

were trying to work out what on earth had just happened to them all. They had no idea. However, they had lost not just a few seconds but hours of time for which they had no conscious memories.

Following this strange incident, the male in the group, who had been the driver, experienced tooth pain and went to the dentist. At the dentist, an unidentified black object fell out of his tooth – despite him having no fillings in that tooth or any other teeth in his mouth.

Following this incident, he reported what had happened to the local authorities. It was not much longer before he found himself receiving visitors in the form of Air Force personnel, who came to him twice. They warned him never speak to of the events that had happened to him. On the same night that his car was on the Highway, a local businessman came forward with a strange story himself. He claimed he had seen a strange craft on the same road as the abducted group's encounter took place. He said it appeared to be huge and the shape of a "child's spinning top." He also saw a UFO as big as a football field. He said that the large craft had a "myriad of lit windows," and was large enough to be a mother ship "capable of transporting hundreds of people."

~~~~

When 26-year-old Bill Herrman, a mechanic living in Charleston South Carolina, first saw luminous objects in the sky, he wasn't too alarmed because he thought they had to be some sort of military aircraft flying out of nearby Charleston Air Force Base. In all, he estimated he had fifteen sightings and forgot most of them, until March 18th, 1978. That particular evening, he came out of his trailer to investigate what he'd seen come down from the sky into a marshy area behind the field by his trailer. He'd seen a "metal disc" approximately 20 meters in circumference, swoop down from the sky above his mobile home.

When he arrived at the location; "Suddenly it was right in front of me. I fell backwards. The next thing I knew there was lights all around me and I felt myself being tugged upward." Just moments later, or so he thought, he found himself coming round in a field, miles from his trailer. Around him, a glowing circle of light was fading away. "I couldn't remember anything. I didn't know where I was. Terrible fear came over me and I sat there crying. I felt dirty. I felt like I had been around something I shouldn't have been around. I can't describe it, but I felt dirty." Faced with something he couldn't explain, he wept.

Sometime after the experience, he underwent hypnosis to try to recover more details about what had happened to him. "I'd tried to run but my legs wouldn't move; it was like I was paralyzed. I couldn't yell. I thought, "Oh God, I'm going to die." He says he was taken inside a craft and placed on "this low examination table" where three strange-looking beings examined him. He said these creatures were just under 5 feet tall and had no hair. Their eyes were black and had no pupils. Their skin was "the colour of marshmallows. Their heads looked like overgrown human foetuses with no ears or hair."

These alarming-looking entities told him: "Don't be

afraid!" He said they were speaking in English, but they spoke without moving their lips. They anticipated his questions and answered them without him asking them. He said they referred to him as "a subject," and he felt certain he was not the first human they had abducted and experimented on.

On the night it happened, he called Deputy Pike Limehouse with the Dorchester Sheriff's Office, who arrived at approximately 1:15 a.m. at the remote area near Summerville, to investigate. The Deputy later told Charleston City Newspaper that he had never seen a man that 'excited' before, as they stood together in the field, under a half-full moon. 'The officer expected the worst, but what he got was the unbelievable.' Herrmann's employer and long-time friend described Bill as a good member of his church, his family, and the community. In the years that followed the disturbing incident, Herrmann started writing pages of notes, in a language he did not know. He said he was channelling messages from the beings that had taken him. Hermann told his local newspaper The Post and Courier that he was sent a strange metal bar sometime after he was taken, from his abductors, and on the bar was the word: "MAN". He said it was only then that the partial memories of something happening to him in the field that night started to come back to him.

Two years later, in a letter to the Newspaper, he declared that the UFO phenomenon was "Satanic in nature and demonic in origin." He was a Baptist, and he said he had found that when he had a second abduction incident by the same beings, when he called out the name of Jesus, they fled. It's interesting to note that, similar to Kelly Cahill's experience with the strange beings, during which she felt they knew the things about her that she wouldn't want her friends and family to know; Bill describes "feeling dirty" – as if these Beings were also delving into all the previous things in Bill's life, that he wouldn't want everyone to know, like all of us have certain things we would prefer to keep to ourselves, private things; sad things for example, or times when we didn't act as good as we could have; why would the 'Aliens' delve into them, bring them into our minds, at our most vulnerable – during the most terrifying moments of our lives - during an 'abduction'?

Or do they project terrible thoughts into our minds? Or did Bill mean something else – something very bad about them instead? And, why is it that quite often, abductees are able to make the 'aliens' scatter and flee upon uttering the name of Jesus? Why are they, or at least some of 'them' afraid of Jesus? What does this tell us of their nature? And what did the entity mean when he told Kelly Cahill's husband, "I am her Father"?

Are these experiences real? And yet, how else can they be explained unless wild dreams? In the case of more than one witness experiencing the same thing, such as in Cahill's case, it's hard to argue that these are nightmares, (given they happen when the person is also not in bed!) Are those who have disappeared and never been seen again, the ones that abductees see in the glass containers or naked lying on the floors of sterile rooms surrounded by creatures worse than the most terrible nightmares; is this where the hundreds of thousands who vanish across the world each year end up?

Australian Kelly Cahill was a housewife and mother of

three, with no interest in spaceships or aliens. "In August 1993, I was driving home from a girlfriend's house in the foothills of the Dandenongs Mountain ranges, (35 km east of Melbourne) driving on Bellegrave Hallam Road and it was just on dusk. I saw, what I thought was round orange lights in the field. It looked unusual to me." Kelly noticed something else. "About a kilometre or so in front of us, about twice the height of the tree tops, we could see this object. It was a light. As we got closer to it, the light seemed to sort of separate and it was actually a row of round lights and they were orange. It appeared like there were silhouettes standing in these round orange circles, like people that you could only see a black outline. I said, "That's people," and the minute I said that, it shot off to the left of us. Within one or two seconds it was gone."

"About a kilometre or two further down the road, as we kept driving, we came across what I thought was a screen or a wall of light across the road. My heart started racing. Adrenaline was sort of pumping through my body, then the next instant we seem to have actually covered a fair distance that I don't even remember covering. It might have been possibly close to a kilometre that I don't remember actually travelling. There was no light there, there was nothing blocking the road now.'

Calhill says it wasn't until several weeks later that she remembered she had actually got out of the car that night. "I saw that there was another car that had pulled up a hundred metres down the road, and I walked around the front of the car, where my husband was standing on the other side and we started walking across the road together. As we were walking across the road, I saw that other people were getting out their car and starting to walk across the road as well, so I was happy that there were other people there who were seeing the same thing that we were, and we walked together to where the fence is. Getting out of the car, all I could think is it's just absolutely amazing and we're seeing something that most people wouldn't get the chance to see in a million lifetimes; then all of a sudden that euphoria changed to absolute horror."

"Right out in front of us was this huge craft. This tall

dark Being just appeared in front of the craft and he was followed by about another seven or eight more that appeared straight behind him. I felt this energy go through me – it was like nothing I've ever experienced before in my life. It was like some sort of low-level frequency that came in waves but it was so dense that I could actually physically feel it going through my body and that feeling absolutely terrified me. It was like I can't even explain the horror that I felt; and I began screaming. A lot of people might have experienced this fear in a nightmare; when you're being chased or something like that, and it's a terror that sometimes can wake you up and it's absolutely horrifying when you're dreaming it; that's exactly what I was feeling while I was totally awake; that sort of terror, as a reality is like a living nightmare. I really think that now I can understand the terror of a wild animal when it's been caught."

"The minute I laid eyes on these things, they came charging across the field. In the three or four seconds it took these beings to cross the hundred and seventy meters between us, all I could do was stand there - not so much physically paralyzed but totally transfixed. There really was no time to do anything else. You're thinking - I've probably got two or three seconds left to live. Halfway across they split up into two groups. Some headed off and the rest came directly towards us. I felt this blow to my solar plexus and I landed flat on my back in the grass, knocked over by something that didn't touch me. It was almost like an electric charge of some sort. It wasn't like a thump; it was like I'd received an electric shock."

"I thought I was going to die. I thought if I don't get up now, I'm never going to; I'm going to pass out and I'm going to die. I'm not going to come back to consciousness, you know, so I pulled myself up into a sitting position and there was like just this black in front of my eyes." The other people who had stopped their car were able to draw sketches of what they had seen that night, and it matched what Cahill sketched – even though they never met each other after the incident. She said the beings that she encountered "were not the usual little gray things that are media propaganda. I found a small red colored equilateral triangle underneath my navel, which I guess in reality provoked only a minor curiosity at the time. It was oddly geometric."

She said that in 1993, flashbacks began to happen to her. Some of these memories were very personal and she felt humiliated by some of them – she found herself being reminded of things she had done in the past and knowing that these were things she would not ordinarily want to share with anyone or wish for anyone to know. She says she knows that these beings were not human. "For some reason, I had expected to see a human when the beings approached, but it was very tall and black. This was not a human - its shape was all wrong." She says she knows that she tried to communicate with the Being. "Big Mistake!! Immediately I was flooded with the most horrifying fear I believe a human is capable of knowing." She knows that she whispered to her husband; "They have no souls."

It's eyes, she said, were like glowing red coals of fire. Then the dark field became filled with many more of these beings, all as tall, all with red eyes of fire. "They had no mouth, no nose or any other facial features. I was transfixed. I could not take my eyes from them. Their energy or power was unfathomable. My mind became a sea of intense confusion, a roaring wind inside my head. It was interfering with my brain and I had to fight it or I was going to die. "They've going to kill us!" she screamed. "They're evil".

When she'd fallen to the floor she became blind, and all she could hear was her husband's voice, in the distance, not close to her anymore. He was shouting "Let me go! Let me go!" A response came from one of the tall dark beings. "We mean no harm to you."Her husband somehow managed to find his voice again and demanded, "Then why did you hit Kelly?" She'd fallen to the floor when she had hit some kind of electrical barrier that was invisible. The tall being replied, "I wouldn't harm her – after all, I am her father." Then the being laughed mockingly. When she still wouldn't shut up screaming, the being said, "Will someone do something about her."

Kelly remembers shouting to the other people who were

also being taken from the field. "Don't believe them! They are evil! They are trying to trick you. They want your souls. They want to steal your souls." Kelly claims that, after this night, the terrifying entities returned to her on at least four more occasions, appearing in her bedroom where she was asleep. They appeared as shadowy cloaked figures. Another woman called 'Glenda,' who had been there that night, who had also been lured out of her car, "had a clear ligature mark around her ankle. It was quite severe bruising and looked like she'd been strapped down to something."

Perhaps the strangest thing about the horrifying ordeal Kelly went through, was when the tall being said; "Will someone do something about her." Doesn't that sound very much like something a human would say? Was there any chance that this experience was perpetrated by the military or government rather than aliens, and yet, how could they manifest in her bedroom in a locked house....?

Kelly says, "Had I glimpsed into another reality? Many followers of religion believe in the invisible world. Could

UFO's be part of this? "I was totally convinced, and I still am, that I was in the presence of something totally diabolical at the very last stage of my conscious recollection."

Chapter Nine

Fallen Angels, the Dragon & The Missing

Kelly Cahill's lasting impression and belief about these beings is that they were something 'diabolical.' In other words, of a daemonic nature - spiritual rather than 'off-planet;' like demons, or Fallen Angels, as did Bill Hermann too, after his encounter. They are "Satanic in nature and demonic in origin," he believes.

While perhaps we could say that it could be possible for underground bases, and bases underwater to potentially exist; there is another intriguing possibility to explain the cause of the missing, the abducted, the drowned and the dead. When L. Savage wrote 'It is necessary to defeat the aliens in the supernatural realm, empowered by sorcery; in this war, the Chaplain is of greater value than the General, as the aliens attack via advanced sorcery,' well, a couple of years ago, a lady called Coral Hull contacted me. She told me she had read my 'In the Woods' books and 'Dead in the Water,' and she felt that she could offer some explanations about what might be happening to the people who go missing and why.

Dr. Coral Hull is a published poet, artist, and PhD in Creative Arts, whose writing has been featured on school curriculum in her native Australia and worldwide. She's had a remarkable life it would seem.

(www.coralhull.com/testimony/fallenangelsexposed/) She had contacted me to say, that having read my books, she would like to offer me permission to write about her story and her insights into the cases and causes of missing people.

"In 2003, I suddenly became very ill, with chronic fatigue syndrome, which left me bedridden. I was diagnosed with Autism. I was experiencing RSPK – Recurring spontaneous psychokinesis. I had suspected for a long time that the phenomenon was coming from an outside source - and a two-way communication was established between them and myself in 2004, through telepathy and channelling. Being into New Age philosophy and a shamanic pagan, I referred to this source as 'angelic beings and guides,' but this MK Ultra was designed and maintained by "The Dragon."

Coral's story is strange, frightening and very curious. "After being saved in 2009, I was to gradually discover I had been raised and groomed by a spiritual non-human entity, a Fallen Angel, leviathan, serpent, part of Satan's hierarchy, who had demons under his command. I refer to him as 'The Dragon.' Selected children, or chosen ones are repeatedly tested and programmed throughout childhood, to ascertain the best way they can be utilized. Unbeknownst to me, my purpose became to promote an anti-Christian agenda through arts and poetry. This was all controlled and monitored by my spiritual handler.

As an infant, I was subjected to MK Ultra Monarch programming – including Alpha, Beta, Theta, Omega, Gamma and Marrionette (Doll) Programming. A number of 'selves' were created to cope with and to potentially fulfil this programming. My situation was different to the 'super-soldier' programs or children who suffer SRA – Satanic Ritual Abuse at the hands of human beings, since my handler and minders were inter-dimensional non-human entities – Fallen Angels and demons with The Dragon impersonating the spirit of God.

Under The Dragon, I am probably best known as a published poet, writer and director of the Thylazine Foundation. She has a BA, MA, and a Doctorate of Creative Arts. She has been published by Penguin Books and won prizes for her poetry. She had the world at her feet, but "After failing to pass a series of 'tests,' my career was terminated." The tests were set by the spiritual 'powers that be;' her handler, the Fallen Angel; The Dragon.

"The Dragon then appears to have gained permission to use me as a personal plaything, referring to me as his 'pet Doll.' During these enchanted years, I went away on a supernatural adventure."

At the time, I had no idea I was in communication with

The Dragon and his demons. From 1999 – 2009, are periods of time that I cannot be fully accounted for. The supernatural phenomenon increased and during this time, a number of deaths occurred in my family and several acquaintances. Grief stricken and needing answers, I became increasingly involved in mediumship and the occult.'

After becoming more involved and immersed in the esoteric world of spirit channelling and mediumship and the occult arts, The Dragon made his presence felt.' She became stalked and controlled, for many years, by this inter-dimensional entity called 'The Dragon,' who entered both her mind, and her physical world.

"He began to show me many images of women being taken or abducted, by other-worldly beings, who were in love with them. In The Dragon's dimension or 'The Second Heavenlies,' he may look like a cherubic, serpent, or dragon. But in this dimension, he was a spirit, a bright orb, or a light source possessing a powerful sub-conscious in this world; physical, and operating within a 3-D reality. I would see him as a ball of light."

Coral's life, for years, was besieged by this Dragon, this inter-dimensional entity, and her life was infiltrated in an attempt to get her to represent them and their dark agenda – these negative entities, the Fallen Angels. "Fallen Angels; manifesting in orbs, demonic cryptids, and fake UFO's," she quotes from the Bible as to their motives; 'The thief cometh not but for to steal and kill, but that they might have life.'

"When placing my UFO stories online," she says, "my phone line was tapped, and my website visited over a period of weeks, by people in the NT (The Northern Territory Government in Australia) and an investigative agency in D.C." This is intriguing. "My car was swooped on by a military helicopter, which also made low swoops over my cottage. I remain under spiritual attack via trials and testing," she says.

"People, many children, have gone missing in the National Parks around the world, under supposed inexplicable circumstances. It is a known but little publicized fact that the name of Jesus stops all supernatural deception and abductions,' she says. 'The name of Jesus stops all fallen angle and demonic attack; whether it be fake UFO or MILAB, shadow men or fairies, bigfoot or dogman."

"We are engaged in a spiritual war that is clearly recognised by the enemy. There are rules of engagement, things the enemy – deadly adversaries who desire our eternal destruction - are not allowed to do in the name of Jesus. A fallen Angel once said to me, "Soon it will be time to harvest."

In order to understand what is happening in the missing cases, we need to be aware that the greater reality is a spiritual reality, unseen by human eyes. This list is for the reader to gain a better understanding of the motivations of the supernatural perpetrators in the missing cases.... Motivation: is their malice toward humans. During a Fallen Angel attack, your environment may appear different; hallucinations, holograms, augmented reality, fake alien/fairy or MILAB.

Motivation; a desire to mislead, confuse, disorient, as in getting lost, mind control, altered states of consciousness, false visions, trances states. A desire to dominate; control, degrade, humiliate humans. A desire to physically hurt humans; injure, cause death, disfigure, maim, mutilate whilst still alive like the cattle mutilations," or, "crushed, burnt, cut, decapitated, dismembered, blood extracted, torn apart etc."

As her list progresses, it become clear and obvious how easily these are all things that appear to happen to those who vanish under inexplicable circumstances in the woods and forests, and how easily there could be an other-worldly group of perpetrators from the 'spirit' world doing this.

The Fallen Angels, she says, have "A desire to lead, lure, chase or herd humans into physical danger so they will physically perish – from dehydration, fatigue, exposure, hypothermia, injury, accident, drowning in a river, swamp or creek, tank, falling off a cliff edge or look-out."

"A desire to see humans falling; represents the original fall of Lucifer and the fallen angels from heaven. A desire to see humans lifted, hanging, or suspended, represents the spirit being out of body, sacrifice, crucifixion of Christ. A desire to see humans drowning or drowned; goes back to God's flood and a desire for revenge on God and the descendants of Noah after the loss of everything that the fallen angles had created. Fallen angles have neither forgotten nor forgiven God for sending the Great Flood."

She continues; "A desire to be worshipped as God; this worship requires the person to fall to the ground into a position of submission or subjugation where they are face-down. This worship also requires the person to remove their shoes/ or for their shoes to be removed."

'Put off your shoes from off your feet, for the place wherein you stand is Holy ground,' God told Moses. The 'Powers and Principalities' who desire to have the due respect shown for their position – just as God did on Mount Saini – to the geographical formations and dimensional vortexes they (these inter-dimensional spiritual predators) reside over or that have been assigned to them by their Fallen Angel commander-in-chief, Satan."

"There is symbolic meaning as to why most people take off their shoes. In these missing cases – nearly all victims have either one or both shoes missing, along with various articles of clothing; on a practical level, the shoes, coats, are removed so they are more prone to hypothermia, or are less likely to run from their abductor – demonic or bigfoot. Or, they may be collected as trophies – The Dragon, a Fallen Angel, once said to me; "All you were was a trophy," after I was saved by Jesus."

"Fallen Angels have utter contempt for human beings, who were created in God's image. To lose a shoe from a foot in biblical terms is to shame someone. It also signifies the transfer of property in Jewish culture of the Old Testament. In many missing cases, it is the symbolic transferring of the property from Christ to the Fallen Angels – and in regard to the human soul, and the symbology, it is that the human being is transferring the property of themselves, their souls, to the fallen angel by the removal of the shoe," says Coral.

For those who doubt spiritual existence, perhaps we can

more easily believe in seeing angels, and being saved by angelic intervention, of stories of people being saved by angles - (I give some examples of these in my book 'Something in the Woods,' of stories where it would seem that people have been miraculously saved from woods and cliffs and mountains and mortal danger - but is it too hard to believe that if these stories are true, of angelic intervention, then couldn't it also be that the stories of being harmed by the counterpart of angels – the fallen angels, are also true?

If we find ourselves calling out to God or Jesus or an angel in personal moments of terror or danger or despair, then surely, so too could we bring ourselves to believe that if they exist so too could their enemies – the fallen ones. Coral Hull's list of the intervention of spiritual entities, wanting humans to be lost, suffer hypothermia, be mutilated, fall off cliffs, drown, take trophies from us like shoes, like inter-dimensional serial killers, for they cannot have what we have – physical bodies and free determination, all in the wish to degrade those they envy – the human – to see their victim lost, frightened, hopeless, and broken. Coral

Hull's thesis would seem to make a lot of very good points. Is it possible that adults and children visiting National Parks, forests and woods, are allowed to become 'prey' or 'sacrifices' to the daemonic 'powers and principalities' that reign over this land....?

Was this next encounter one of the Fallen Angel's Coral Hull talks of, in the form of the Fey? (And this takes place in Manchester, where multiple men have been found dead in the canals.) George, a British man who practices witchcraft (https://www.youtube.com/watch?v=-BmM57PbdYA) says; "I came to a decision I should tell you. You could get a little freaked out, but this genuinely happened. We're going to speak about my experiences with 'the little people,' as they prefer to be called now. I used to work at a club in the gay village in Manchester. I used to work every Sunday night and it was at a place called 'Crews.' Now Crews closed normally around 5:00 in the morning; however they close 4:00 on Sundays, and sometimes to get home you had to walk, but then I suddenly realized that I had £20 in my bank account, so I knew I had to go to the cash machine to get some cash out.'

'So anyway, I've walked out of the gay village and over the crossroads and I was standing at the cash machine and this man walked toward me, and he was beautiful; absolutely - stunning. The weirdest thing is, I can't actually remember what his face looked like – I just remember his eyes and his hair. He had jet black hair a little like mine and the most beautiful crystal-clear blue eyes I have ever seen in my life.'

'This man was stunning, and he walked up to me and he was Irish, and he said; "Excuse me," and I was like "Yeah?" He was like; "Where can I get a gal around here?" I was like laughing to myself because I was like 'Whoa - I'm gay, how am I gonna be able to tell you where to get a girl from! and I said; "Nah, I'm really sorry, I don't know, mmm maybe if you head towards that direction," and I sent him a way basically away from the gay village, because he was looking for a gal. So, I went to the cash machine and didn't think anything of it.

The cash machine said, 'This machine is out of order,' so I walked back towards the gay village. I was hungry,

I was tired, and I wanted to get home, and I pass this club that was open, and who is standing on the crossroads but my little Irish friend - now at the time I was just like 'Whoa - that's weird, because the guy had defeated physics - it freaks me out and he actually did as well - there is no other way - it's not physically possible to get to where he was in such a little amount of time unless he got to the road, hops on a motorbike and parked it up and runs to where I was!'

'So, it was weird, and then he goes; "Excuse me," as if he'd never seen me before. He went; "Do you know where I can get a girl around here?" and I was like; "Look, I really don't know," and I was freaked. I went; "I really don't know but you're in the gay village!" And he went; "Oh!" and I said, "Look, you should go back the way I sent you." And he went; "Ok."

So anyway, I headed towards another cash machine which was where I was already heading towards when I saw him on the crossroads again, so I saw him and I walked the opposite way. And again, the only way you can get to where I was going was if you literally went halfway around town. So, anyway, I stood there at this second Cash Machine and once again, it said, 'Out of order,' and I was like; what is going on here? - something is not right, something in the air, it didn't feel right, and all of a sudden, I heard; "Excuse me," like that, and I hate literally even speaking about it and now I'm going over all cold because it's terrifying. I turn around. I said to him; "No." like that, and we just stopped and we're staring at each other and he went; "Do you know where I can get a gal around here, could you please tell me where I can get a gal. I want a gal."

'And I just freaked, and I was so so petrified, and I just thought; this is weird, and I just looked at him and I thought; you're not human. This thought went through my head and I just thought; Christ – you're actually not human, and he looked at me dead in the eye and he said; "Isn't it a weird city. Isn't this town a weird town." And I was just like, "Look, I don't know who you are but please leave me alone because you're frightening me." I was speaking to him as if he was a spirit. This guy had defeated physics like two times. It was so strange, so bizarre, and he didn't look human, and he was beautiful but too beautiful to be human even though I can't remember what he looked like. It was so weird. I just went, "Look, just go!"

He set off the other way, the complete opposite way, opposite to me, and so I came to the decision "F... this. I'm going to walk home. As freaked out as I was, I was walking straight home. Well on the way I pass MacDonald's, so thinking I'll just get some food with my card because I'm so hungry – bearing in mind the guy had walked the other way, well, I get to MacDonald's and as I looked through the window he was there, and he looked me dead in the eye, and he was like, "Oh! There you are!" and he gets up and is running towards me.'

'Well I pegged it - I've never ran so fast. I was crying. I was literally crying because the fact is this guy defeated physics. It was so weird, there was something in the air, and this is gonna sound crazy, but I don't care; he was not human. He was not human at all. A couple of weeks after this had occurred, I was walking home and I passed the crossroads and there, just standing on this crossroads – is a man – just staring at me, standing still, his head cocked to one side, frozen, and it was the weirdest thing I've ever come across – the whole experience was weird – but it kept happening – the same man at the crossroads – just staring, not saying a word. This is what people get confused with and don't often understand with fairies or the little people – is that they don't only live in woods or nature – they adapt their environment around them, just like we have, so you can get somebody who may look like a businessman and so he may carry a briefcase; but it isn't sometimes necessarily human - they're just trying to fit into the world like us.

Basically, fairies have a habit of kidnapping people and I believe this man was trying to find a woman – not for sexual reasons – I may sound crazy; but after that, I was carrying iron keys around with me for a good while cos I was just petrified. Traditionally iron keys have been used throughout folklore to repel evil. Not particularly sure why but it's a very old practice. That is my experience of the 'little people.' Some of them are very very strange, because they are not human, they don't think like humans. They are completely separate beings. Not all of them are 'fluffy bunny' and nice – some are, but not all are. Yeah, he definitively frightened me, even before the ball dropped, so to speak. There was a presence about him, the kind that if he were hiding in a room you'd still know he was there. The second man could have been him too. He was standing at different crossroads each time. I don't know what he wanted her for (here he means a girl, when the 'man' kept asking him, where could he find a girl.) "I'm not sure I wanna know! lol ... I know that the Fae are notorious for being kidnappers."

While this man's experience may sound incredibly strange, I myself have had a very similar experience of a man who defied physics while out in a bar one night, who did not seem human, and who felt like a threat to my very soul. Anthropologist W. Y. Evans-Wentz, who claimed to have had encounters with the Fairy Folk in the early 1900's, once wrote; 'The folk are the grandest I have ever seen. They are far superior to us, and that is why they are called the gentry. They are not a working class, but a military-aristocratic class, tall and noble-appearing. They are a distinct race between our own and that of spirits, as they have told me. "We could cut off half the human race, but would not," they said, "for we are expecting salvation."

'I knew a man whom they struck down with paralysis. Their sight is so penetrating that I think they could see through the earth. They have a silvery voice, quick and sweet. They take the whole body and soul of young and intellectual people who are interesting, transmuting the body to a body like their own. I asked them once if they ever died, and they said, "No; we are always kept young." You are changed to one of them and live with them for ever. They are able to appear in different forms. One once appeared to me, and seemed only four feet high, and stoutly built. He said, "I am bigger than I appear to you now. We can make the old young, the big small, the small big."

~~~~

But what did this next man encounter....? Of Coral Hull's account of Fallen Angels appearing as bizarre cryptids, could this have been one...? A man called Paul from Orange, Virginia, claims to have had a very strange encounter. He phoned in to tell a late-night radio show about it; "This happened to me last fall 2017. I was out back, sitting on the patio having a cigarette, talking to my friend on a cell phone. It was about 10 at night and very dark. The yard goes back really steep down to the lake here, and there's a lot of woods and brush in between, and it's pretty thick. Well, suddenly I heard something running across the yard, right through all the thick brush. I said, 'What was that? - something just ran through the yard!' It was big, whatever it was."

"I couldn't figure why it ran - where it ran when it could have been a little further down by the lake, where it had free run, because it's all open down there. I said, 'Maybe it's a deer, I guess.' But I've never seen a deer here in this spot before. It just seemed like a weird time for it to be running. Anyway, I kind of forgot about it. I kept talking to my friend. Suddenly I hear a noise down by the dock. I was like, 'There it is again.' For some reason, my first thought was there's some kids playing around down there. Anyway, I got up and I went running over towards the stairs to go down to the dock. They're steep stairs and when I get to the top of them and I look down, there's this thing running up the stairs towards me and I was just in shock."

"It was like, it was a person, but it had a deer head. And it was running up the stairs so fast, it was crazy that it could even move that fast and it was staring right at me. And I'm just standing there and I'm staring at it. And it had red eyes. It actually had red eyes."

"It ran right up to me. It kept staring me in the eyes and I was staring right back at its eyes, just kind of in shock, I guess. When it got right up to me, it actually said something which I don't know what it said. I just know it said something like four or five syllables real fast. It seemed like it said words, but I don't know what they were. And then it ran.... it just kept running and ran right by me. I could have touched it.... it was within inches of me. The stairway is only four feet across."

"I hardly told anybody about this because it was just the craziest thing I have ever seen. It was moving so fast that when I thought about it later, I was like, man, it was almost like in a different dimension or something. That's all I could think. It was a being that had a human body and a deer head. And the antlers weren't like the deer around here. They weren't like the white-tailed deer here. They were more spindly. They were spindly and there was more, a lot more, like ties or branches than normal. I think it was human from the neck down but to be honest with you, I didn't look down at his legs. I was just staring at his face while it was coming at me, you know. I didn't notice any kind of clothes. I mean, honestly, that thing locked its eyes on mine and I was locked on its eyes."

What on earth was that....?

As readers may know, from the beginning when I first went on Coast to Coast Am to talk about 'Something in the Woods,' I have been collecting accounts of what seem to be sightings of an 'Invisible Predator' which at times seems entirely naked to the eyes and at other times appears as shimmers like ripples, and most who have seen it can think of nothing else to compare it to other than the entity in the 'Predator' movie. Perhaps the movie is not fiction at all....

Many people over the years have since contacted me to relate their terrible fear upon seeing this nebulous horrifying entity that never fully shows itself but strikes terror into the heart of those who encounter it. Is this entity a Fallen Angel, not fully manifest...?

Makaya says she was walking the dog with her dad when they noticed something in the brush. 'If you've ever seen "Predator", you know how he can appear clear sometimes?   This thing was clear like that – except it was human–shaped. I know it wasn't a hallucination; since it made the brush shake, it couldn't have been an illusion, and my dad shinned the flashlight at it and it turned and looked at us."

"My heart was pounding. We just kept walking and didn't say anything for about ten seconds and then we both said at the same time; "Did you see that?" My heart was beating, I was panicking – the thing actually interacted with the physical world; when it hit a branch and the branch shook! It couldn't have been an illusion. It was camouflage, but you could see an outline, and it was moving. It was not a trick of the eye – tricks of the eye do not leave physical markers."

Aanica says; "I really don't know what to call it, yet my boyfriend and I were camping in 2008, just sitting around the lake and talking, and I looked at the woods and it was there, sitting against a tree, legs stretched and crossed, just watching us. I was scared to death, so I just ignored it – and then when I did look back, it was gone. It did not care that I saw it. Very creepy how it was just there watching. It has camo that is all over it like a skin. It blends in right in front of your face."

In 2014, 'Greg' from North Carolina called into a radio show to tell of his unsettling experience in Tennessee in 1994; "I was living in Nashville. I didn't drink or do drugs. It was about 3 in the afternoon. I was out walking the dog and I could feel something watching me. I started looking directly at the woods in front of me and I couldn't see anything but I could hear leaves rustling in the trees, so I started looking up toward the top of the trees. I had very good eyesight at the time. I saw something crouched down in the tops of the trees. The only way I could describe it, and I don't even know if the movie had come out yet, so I didn't know anything about the Movie 'Predator' where they saw

194

that invisible creature, yet you could see the outline of everything but you could see right through it, and it was sitting up in the very tops of the trees where it wouldn't hold the weight of a man by any means.

This thing was as big as a man. I just stood there looking at it and then I let go of the dog and I took off at a dead run toward this thing. It started running across the tops of the trees — it ran the length of a football field in just no time, really fast. I don't know how it was running across the tops of the trees, but I know what I saw. After, I thought about it; what in the world are you doing chasing this thing! I stopped. And it stopped, about the length of a football field away from where it was and it turned around and looked at me. It scared the hell out of me, I know that. I never told anybody because people would think I was crazy.

In another account, 'First off, I don't do drugs, drink, and as far as I know I'm sane. I don't believe in aliens. I have a college degree. Yesterday I was walking my dog; I'm in the country and the woods are all along that road. Just off the path I saw something that disturbed me; the only way to describe it is it was Predator-like.

My dog didn't notice it apparently. We were shaded under the cover of the trees, with no broken streaks of light. It was a clear sky anyway so it wasn't the sun and it wasn't shadows of leaves. I investigated all of the possibilities. It was off the ground by about a foot and it was shadow-like. As though holographic in nature. It was running into the woods. At first I thought it was like a sort of enormous snake but I realized there was no solid form. It really looked like a scene out of the film, although I haven't seen it for a few years, where you see the feet moving like a holograph, as though superimposed over the plants and leaves. It was the strangest thing I have ever seen. I saw the plants moving where it went. There were no sounds of wildlife but I noticed that after it ran the sounds began to come back. One thing is a lot of things are found dead on this road. There's always road kill. What did I see? Was it an illusion I just couldn't figure out? Did I see a different dimension?'

And a man I have spoken with wrote, 'In Colorado here seen something similar a few years back; only this one settled into a cottonwood tree next to my house. There was nothing there to be seen but it was active. All day it broke branches, snapping them from the tree and throwing or dropping them down, regular. A friend came over and I told him and we sat outside looking. There were no animal sounds; deathly silent, not even insects. No wind. Every couple of minute's branches snapped, forming a pile on the ground. Bolstered by my friend I walked the sixty feet to the tree, but staying about thirty feet from it. I could see nothing, then a branch about fifteen feet long got thrown in my direction! I backed off quick and said a prayer. It stopped immediately?!

About a year later I learnt by chance about a man and his wife walking by a creek who became aware of something moving through the tree tops, breaking off branches as it went along - they said they saw a 'shimmering' aka Predator-which I didn't. Another very weird thing; we have people occasionally go missing here, in the mountains. One man went missing several years ago. They found his skeleton with his backpack. The Skeleton was intact, but the skull was missing.'

It's interesting to note that he claims in his case, it stopped after he said a prayer. Very similar to the plethora of accounts of people who say they've had encounters with demonic and reptilian entities, and have found that by praying aloud it has forced them to leave. Though not successful in every case, in the majority of cases it does seem to work. Does this give some kind of clue as to the origins of these invisible beings?

In this last account, 'A friend and I were driving around a backroad in Hayesville, North Carolina, back around 1994. I saw something hard to describe. It came out of the high grass to the right of our vehicle and streaked across the road. It appeared to be bi-pedal, maybe 3 feet tall, and incredibly fast, and transparent; weird, like it was made of heat ripples. Whatever the hell it was, it made me slam the brakes. We watched in awe as it violently disturbed the surrounding foliage, scared birds and vanished into the treeline.'

In Slavic Lore of eastern Europe, 'the Leshy' are male woodland Spirits. They can appear as tall men or with a tail and hooves and horns, but they also have the ability to change size and shapeshift into any form – be it animal or plant, but it is said they can shrink themselves to the height of a blade of grass or grow to the size of the tallest tree. They like to lead people astray. They have horrible cries, but they can also imitate a human voice and are said to often lure lost travellers to their caves. They like to kidnap humans.

What was this next creature...? It began on the evening of November 17th, 1974, when deer hunter Ernest Smith was driving alone along a quiet road on bald mountain in the state of Washington. In the beam of his headlights he suddenly saw something so strange it makes no sense at all.

"It was the size of a horse, covered in scales and standing on four rubbery legs with suckers like octopus tentacles. The head was shaped like a football with an antenna sticking out of it. It gave off a green iridescent glow, like a neon sign in the fog."

Several other eye-witnesses saw the same thing. Mr.

and Mrs. R. Ramsbaugh also claimed they saw the same monster too. They were driving along the road when they saw "a dull glow near the side of the road." The husband slowed down the car to take a better look. They too saw this strange iridescent glow, followed by a horse-tentaclled-rubbery monster. Sheriff William Wiester was called to investigate – after a number of reports were made that evening. However, researcher at the time, Jim Brandon, claimed, "Heavily armed military with no insignia" descended on the mountain, sealing off the road and conducting a search."

~~~

An M. Giebler sent her strange story to the Rocky Mountain Sasquatch Organization. In August 2014, she was on a camping trip in Bald Mountain with her husband and five grandchildren. They'd eaten lunch before they arrived, so that afternoon they were all heading out on a hike. While they were all gathering to get ready to set off, one of her grandchildren said suddenly, "Look at that running on the hill!"

The grandmother says she looked up, "And I saw what I thought was a large man in a black jogging suit with a hoodie, sort of jogging down an incline." Her husband was in the bathroom, and she called out to him. "I called out that something must have happened; a man was running down this steep trail, and maybe someone was hurt."

At the same time, it had begun to rain, and they'd not set up their tent yet, so they all went inside the trailer to shelter from the rain.

"We were watching this, what I thought was a person. He was still going down this ridge. My granddaughter started getting scared, and it was at that moment I realized what we were watching. I said, "He's watching us." It just stood there looking back at us. Then, after a few minutes, it looked like it had sat down. I decided to try and spot it with a telescope we'd taken to look at the starts later – but everything was a blur and we didn't pack binoculars. The girls were uneasy and that night we slept in the trailer."

"I was still unsure what we saw, but I didn't sleep well that night. Next day, when we got up, we were the only camp there – which we thought was strange. Anyway, when I saw some hikers on the ridge, I knew it wasn't a regular person we'd been watching the day before. He was twice as tall and even his thighs were enormous compared to those hikers. We decided it was time to find another campsite elsewhere. We didn't talk about it as we didn't want to scare the kids, but was I freaked out about the whole ordeal. We stayed one more night and came home. We didn't go camping again all year."

What exactly did she see....?

Chapter Ten

Missing in the Wild Highlands

'Mountain rescue teams are searching for a man who disappeared from Fort William to Tillicoultry,' wrote the Scottish Newspapers in September 2017. 'Dozens of volunteers have been combing the countryside to locate a 63-year-old man who vanished during a 100-mile cycle ride' in hilly terrain in the Scottish Highlands. 'Tony Parsons set off on a bicycle from Fort William to his home in Tillicoultry, Clackmannanshire, on Friday September 29th and has not been seen since,' reported Scotland's Daily Record Newspaper.

Anthony 'Tony' Parsons caught the train north to the Highland's town earlier in the day with the intention of cycling over 100 miles back home, in what was said to be a personal challenge. He had cycled the ascent to Glencoe, famous for its stunning, awe-inspiring wilderness scenery of rugged hills, mountains and moorlands and the location for James Bond's return to his ancestral home in the movie 'Skyfall.' Parsons had cycled forty miles to the Bridge of Orchy Hotel, a popular stopping point along the famous West Highlands Way, a long-distance hiking route through the Highlands but one with few houses and few residents. Here, a cairn offers sensational views over Loch Tulla and towards the peaks of the Black Mount as well as back to the Beinn Dorain range.

There is a single-track railway station there; but by the time Mr Parsons had reached there, the last train for the night would have left already. A witness saw him leaving the Bridge of Orchy heading south on the A82. The A82 is the road along which coaches and travellers use to reach the Highlands from Glasgow. It was Midnight when the witness saw him. The next village was approximately 10 km away. There is a possible alternate route to reach the village of Tyndrum - it's a hiking route but not suitable for cars. This section of the Way closely follows the line of the West Highland Railway.

It can be travelled by bicycle, but to get onto this route, he would have needed to access it prior to reaching the Bridge of Orchy and given that he was seen heading south after the Bridge of Orchy, he would have to have doubled back on himself. If the witness is correct in that they saw him cycling away from the hotel heading south and the police said they found the sightings credible, then it seems unlikely he would have then turned around and double backed on himself. It's also not a route advertised on road signs.

There was also a later unconfirmed sighting of him a little further on south on the same A82 road. There were no confirmed sightings of Parsons at the next village he had been heading to. A service station there had cctv but according to PhD researcher Sean Leavey, this did not capture him passing by on his bicycle and the CCTV camera was pointed toward the road. Police also made no mention of him being seen on camera cycling past the service station.

Mr Parsons was last seen leaving Bridge of Orchy at around 11.30pm that evening, then a witness saw him just outside the village as he cycled south along the A82. He was wearing a red waterproof jacket, beige combat trousers, a silver and grey cycling helmet, fingerless gloves and hiking boots, as well as a high visibility vest. He had with him a silver and blue backpack. His mountain bike was yellow with black handlebars. He was described by Scottish police as 5ft 9 inches, of stocky build, with short dark hair and glasses.

Police began the search for him and this involved Mountain rescue teams from Killina, Oban, and Arrochar, as well as Coastguard teams. Parsons had once been in the Royal Navy serving on a Polaris submarine, but the feat he was attempting at the age of 63 was quite challenging even for hardy cyclists; what many people also couldn't understand was why had he set out at 11.30 pm in pitch dark to ride so far home. The bicycle ride he was undertaking was something he had set for himself as a challenge. Many cyclists would agree however, that the home-bound leg of his journey was perplexing – very few would have set out to do what he was attempting, although he was doing it to raise money for charity.

"He was just a good decent man," former navy-man and good friend John Pritchard told Scottish reporters. "I've known Tony for over 30 years. We were in the Navy together, and then we lived in the same area and ended up at the same rugby club. He was a solid guy – a good guy who would do you a favour any time he could. If he could help you, he would. It doesn't surprise me that he was doing this ride for charity – that was Tony. It's incredibly disappointing that nobody has either seen anything or if they have, they never came forward to say they've seen anything."

Extensive searches of the West Highland Way were made by the coastguard and mountain rescue teams in the days after his disappearance. Police said there had been nothing to suggest anything suspicious had happened to him. "We have not uncovered any evidence at all of any criminality through the extensive searches and inquiries we have conducted," said Chief Inspector Drew Sinclair. "We have traced his movement to the Bridge of Orchy hotel and then a confirmed sighting about ½ a mile south of the hotel from a lorry driver. From there, there's been absolutely no confirmed sightings of him or the bike."

This statement by the Chief Inspector was being made on the 1-year anniversary of the former navy man's disappearance. "It has been an agonising year for his wife and family," said the Inspector, "Without answers about where their husband, dad and grandfather is."Dozens of volunteers had joined the professional organisations looking for him. A police helicopter went out using thermal imaging, but this was not until a couple of days later after he was reported missing – by that time, it would probably have been too late to detect a heat signature. It's possible, because of the challenging route, he may at times even disembarked and walked with his bike. If he had perished out there in the Highlands, why had no hikers, cyclist or cars on the road that runs through the Highlands, seen his body, his belongings or his bicycle?

Had he been victim of an accident? Did a car or truck hit him, then hide his body or bury it on the Highlands, along with his bike and belongings? Yet cadaver dogs had found no scent of his body. "Since Tony was reported missing, numerous officers have assisted with the search activity which has been supported by specialist resources including the Dog Unit and Mountain rescue teams, specialist horses and coastguards. The area Tony was last seen was popular with visitors – I would appeal to anyone who may have seen any piece of clothing similar to what Tony was wearing," said the Inspector.

To date, very curiously, still no trace of him has been found on the moorlands of the Scottish Highlands....

Chapter Eleven

'America's most bizarre unsolved mystery.'

It's been called America's most bizarre unsolved mystery.The unexplained disappearance of the Jamison family of Oklahoma in October 2009, is a mystery which seemingly involves zombie-like trances, witches, fighting demons, a bundle of money, and the vanishing of a family in the remote landscape of the Latimer Mountains. For over 3 years, missing person's posters had been circulated, asking if local people had got any clues as to what might have happened to Bobby Jameson, his wife Sherilynn and their 6-year-old daughter Madison. Only the most cryptic of clues had been left behind when they abruptly vanished without any warning. Sheriff Beauchamp, leading the investigation, summed it up, saying: 'A lot of investigators would love to have as many leads as we do. The problem is they point in so many different directions.'

The family were last known to have been alive on October 8th, 2009. On that day, the family left their home in Eufaula, Oklahoma in their white pick-up truck, and headed out to the remote Red Oak Mountain area apparently looking for somewhere to move to, and with the intention of looking at some land that was for sale. The drive to the location where their truck was found has been described as treacherous and hard. It required a seven-mile journey up a small mountain with many dirt roads until you reach a plateau which was created for a Well site. Above this and beyond is the bluff where the land for sale is situated, that the family were heading to.

Investigators believe the family reached this spot, because religious graffiti such as "Jesus will save you" was found spray painted on an abandoned truck – and this matched graffiti scribbles found at their home on a large storage container they'd purchased to move to the wilderness with and live in. The abandoned junk vehicle had satanic messages written on it and Sherilyn had written over the messages with 'God Loves You' and 'Peace'.

On October 16th, a couple on ATV's came across their pick-up truck on the dirt road which led to the Well site, close to the area where they were going to look for the land for sale, and where the graffiti was found.

The truck was locked and inside of it, the family's dog was close to death from dehydration. Investigators also discovered the family's cell phones inside the truck, along with a very large amount of cash; $32,000, to be precise. One of their cell phones showed a photo taken of Madison, the daughter, that investigators believed had been taken there. The family were no-where to be seen though, and any tracks to indicate where the family had gone after disembarking from their truck, were not visible.

Wherever they'd gone, they'd left behind their jackets, all the money, their phones and their dog. It didn't appear they had planned on being outside of their vehicle for very long. Their truck had been facing toward the exit of the plateau, as though they had turned around and were ready to leave and drive back home.

After relatives realized they had not returned from their day excursion on the 8th, an enormous search effort had been organised, with hundreds of volunteers and troopers from the Oklahoma Highway Patrol. Agents from the FBI also arrived. In all, Newspapers quoted '330 volunteers set out to look for them.'

Searchers combed the area on foot, on ATV's, by air, and on horses, but they found nothing; even with the 16 teams of tracking dogs that had been brought in. Search teams scanned every part of the vicinity scrupulously. Had they got lost in the wilderness? Or had something far more sinister happened to them?

The Sheriff, a former U.S. Army Ranger, said his mind was consumed by questions and theories during the searches. "Throughout this whole process I've found myself going back and forth as to what might have happened," Israel Beauchamp said. "I'm at my wit's end. I asked for all the help I could get. FBI agents; private investigators who contacted me."

If it had been straight forward foul play, surely the

perpetrators would have stolen the money? - There was over $30,000 in cash in the vehicle. But a remote, rugged and quiet landscape is not the most obvious choice for a robber to lie in wait, hoping to find a family to rob – unless they knew them. But the money wasn't stolen.

A man who lived a quarter mile from where the pickup was found, was the last known person to see them. He was questioned. He said he saw no-one else in the vicinity. The man who owned the land they wanted to take a look at, was thought to have been one of the last people to speak to Bobby, and he described him as being 'upbeat and friendly' and said they spoke for quite some time, Bobby asked for the GPS directions for the land, and told the landowner that he had a blackberry phone and he declined the man's offer to meet them to take them to show them the plot of land. Bobby was confident that he would find it.

It appeared that they did indeed find it; but where were they now? Had they wondered off, and got lost? Many have wondered, was it a drug deal gone bad? –

because of the money found. Were the parents drug users? Was it simply a criminal case, or was there something much deeper to this?

The County Sheriff said it could even have been done by "The Mexican Mafia; They could have done it," that's a theory, because Bobby's dad was linked to allegedly the Mexican Mafia and they had burned one of his businesses down in Oklahoma City." Bobby's father died of natural causes in December 2009. At the time of the family's disappearance he was estranged from his son, according to Investigators, and in his Will he left everything to his grandchild Madison, leaving his son out. His dad, Bobby claimed, once hit him with his vehicle, and said the whole family were in terror of him, when he filed a court petition against him. He said his father had threatened to kill them. A protective order however was dismissed by a judge. Bobby's father, Bob, had an alibi – he'd been sick and hospitalized at the time of the family's disappearance.

Bobby's uncle said Bobby's father would simply not do something so bad as to kill his own son. 'I'm pretty sure he was not capable of being involved in that;" he said, adding that with regards to their disappearance; "Nothing makes any sense. It has me puzzled." Bobby was, at the time of his disappearance, suing his father, claiming he was owed property after working for free for his father, but he and his wife had also filed to sue the school where Madison went, after a swing had hit her in the playground. The couple were, it seems, litigious. Sheriff Beauchamp said Law enforcement's investigation into the lives of the Jamieson's after they vanished had led him to believe they may have been scammers.

But there were more odd things about the couple's personal life. Sherilyn had apparently told her neighbours she was a witch and she was going to cast spells on them. In the house, there were a lot of books on spiritual and religious guidance. However, her sister says this was more of a joke, in that if she let her neighbours think she was a witch, it might get them to leave her alone, and she said she and Sherilyn would jokingly gift each other witch-books and leave them lying around the house.

On the other hand, Sherilyn had 3 cats that all died, and she was convinced her neighbours had done it. She spray-painted warnings that she was a witch - so don't hurt her cats, on the storage container on their property. She suffered from bipolar disorder and it was said that she did not always take her meds. She also left behind a journal in the vehicle. She had written about her husband; 'You are a very toxic person, you need to find happiness, you contaminate everything that you're around. It breaks my heart and saddens my soul that you have turned into the monster that you are. I would not wish my daughter to be raised in foster care because of you being in prison or attempted murder and her mother dead.' However, just 3 days before the family disappeared, she wrote that her husband Bobby was 'A genius man with special gifts, and a loving and tender soul, all my love and always forever.'

Sheriff Beauchamp said that, rather strangely, "They were certainly a family obsessed with death,'" after a letter discussing death had been found at the couple's home. It gets stranger. Oklahoma's Red Dirt News reported that Bobby had been reading a "Satanic Bible" for help with natural remedies to guard himself and his family from the bad spirits or demons who were plaguing him. He had visited local Pastor Corey Brandon with his wife. The Pastor said Sherilyn told him, "She could talk to the dead and added that her daughter also had the same power." Sherilyn said the spirits of a long-dead family lived with them and that their daughter Madyson spoke with the youngest apparition.

Bobby had asked the Pastor how he could obtain "special bullets" that would enable him to kill the demons that were terrorizing the family. He said he saw Spirits on the roof of their house, with wings. He too kept a journal; '2-4 am: Spirits walking on the roof.' Niki Shenold, Sherilyn's best friend told the Newspaper, 'In all seriousness, that house was haunted. I don't want to sound crazy, but whenever I went there I felt a horrible presence, I would leave feeling so down and depressed. Once, I was in the living room and this sort of grey mist descended down the stairs. It really scared me. She told me on a couple of occasions, Bobby – who was such a gentle man - would suddenly come at her and his eyes would be completely dead and black, like he was possessed. Sherilyn would leave notes round the house, saying, "Get out Satan," and stuff like that. It was her way of dealing with things.'

As people in the area speculated and tried to understand what had happened to the family, an edition of The Oklahoman headlined the story in a very surprising way. The mother of missing Sherilyn Jamison was telling the Newspaper that her daughter "Was on a cult's hit-list."

Sherlyn's friend Niki also said she was contacted by this anonymous woman who made terrifying claims. The woman who phoned her said that she had once been involved with a white supremacist group and that Bobby and Sherilyn were on their "hit list". Her mother said they were on a "hit list" too but she called the group behind it a "Religious Cult" located in South-Eastern Oklahoma.

After 'Investigation Discovery' aired a special tv show featuring the strange case of the Jamison family, Nikki claims she received a telephone call from this anonymous woman who said that she had ended her own involvement with a white supremacist group that kept a book of names of people who had been a problem for them, and this woman said that after she would see names in this book, when she got home she would look up these names on the internet to see if they had disappeared or died. The woman made the terrifying claim that on many occasions, the names she would look up would turn out to be cases where they had disappeared; that these names led her to multipole multiple missing person's cases, including the Jamison's. Was she legit?

Her friend also said that the lodger who lived with the family, a handy-man, had told them he was a white-supremacist and that he should probably kill a person like Sherilynn (who had Native-American ancestry.) Sherilynn's reaction to his alarming statement was to grab her gun and throw him off their property. The handyman Kenneth Bellows was cleared of any wrongdoing by the FBI in this case. He was in jail at the time of their disappearance.

Sherilynn's mother insisted her daughter was targeted by a religious cult. Curiously, approximately a month before the disappearance of the Jamison family, there was also the case of Pastor Carol Daniels, who was found horrifically murdered in her Church nearby. The local D.A. Mr Burns said of the crime scene that it was "The most horrific he'd ever seen," but he wouldn't go into details as to why. Her mutilated body though was found behind the Church Altar in a crucifix pose, obviously suggesting a link to Satanic ritual. Her killer or killers have never been found. Was it staged to look like a Satanic ritual? Did she simply fall and land in that position, as though laid out on a cross? Or, was she deliberately posed like that?

Her autopsy report shows multiple small superficial knife cuts on her body – a sure sign of satanic ritual; or, was it someone wanting to make it look like that? Whichever the case, her killer or killers had seemed to be in no rush; they had not appeared to be in fear that they would be disturbed or caught. They were calm. Could the Pastor's horrific murder tie-in to the Jamison's disappearance? Apart from the husband and wife's obsession with witchcraft, death, demons and spirits, and her mother's belief they were killed by a religious cult, there was no actual evidence to show it was related.

County Sheriff Robby Brooks said in an interview, 'I believe they were probably high on drugs, high on methamphetamine at the time that they went up to visit the property, that they got out of their car and they wandered off into the mountains.' He asserts that, from the intelligence he gathered, both parents were frequent methamphetamine users, taking drugs every day. Sherilynn's mother Star, and her best friend Nikki, say this is not true. Her mother says she used to look after the child when her daughter's depression got worse, although she also said she had been estranged from the family in the last few months because of her daughter's 'emotional problems.' Her friend, who used to have a problem with Meth herself, says she could tell Sherilynn was not taking drugs leading up to their disappearance. Who is right? The best friend or the intel gathered by the Sheriff?

Her friend says no meth was found in their abandoned truck or in their home, and in fact their house had been expensively renovated and was well-maintained. She adds that the day before they disappeared, Bobby had been looking at schools in the area for their daughter to start attending. Prior to this, the child had been withdrawn from school so that they could home-tutor her, perhaps in line with their vision of moving to the wilderness to live in the container. Some sources say they were moving because they could no longer afford to live in their home.

The husband and wife were also keen, it was said, to live a more self-contained life 'off the grid.' The $32,000 was believed to have been a part-settlement from a serious car accident Bobby had suffered from. This reportedly left him crippled with constant pain and both he and Sherilynn were actually on disability. Bobby could not walk more than a few metres without having to stop because of the pain. How did they walk off far enough not to be found by multiple searches?

Her friend says something is very wrong with the way

they disappeared, and uses as evidence for this, the photo taken of Madison up on the mountain before they vanished. She claims the daughter looks terrified. She is not looking directly into the camera and has her arms folded across her chest. Is she terrified or isn't it just simply an innocent stance of a child who doesn't feel like having her photo taken? "That's not her smile, that's not her face when she's happy,' claims Sherilynn's best friend. The implication then is that someone was with them, forcing them to do things, and had done away with them, but how? And where? The searchers could find no tracks to follow.

A security camera they had installed, had recorded footage at their home, and the camera was apparently installed by the family because of their concerns of the "spiritual attacks" they were experiencing. The footage taken just before they disappeared is very strange. It shows both adults packing up their truck with many large items, and they are walking around at times in rather a zombie-like trance state, as though they are not quite there, as though they are disorientated, prior to their departure. Or was it fear? Were they being forced into doing this by someone? Were they being compelled to do something by the spirits who were supposedly communicating with them? Was this a supernatural intrusion? Was a 'voice' telling them to do this? Or was this simply the effect of drugs?

In the video footage, some say it looks like they are carrying items to the car, and then returning the same items back to the house! They also appear to change clothes while packing up the car, which doesn't seem to make any sense. During this time, a brown briefcase was loaded into the car, and this stayed in the car, however; it was not found in their abandoned truck. What was in this briefcase and where did it go? Why would they leave their dog in the car, their jackets, their phones and, all that money, unless they only intended to be outside of the car for a few minutes? Why could no tracks be found? Bobby had serious constant pain from in his back from his car accident. Sherilyn had a bad shoulder that caused pain. Both were on disability. Bobby could not walk more than a few metres without having to stop because of the pain. How did they walk off far enough not to be found by multiple searches?

Then, in November 2013, the skeletal remains of the family were found by deer hunters about four miles from their truck. This was extremely odd because the Jamison father could not walk more than a few metres without severe pain, and Sherilynn had chronic pain in her neck and shoulder; yet they were found on the opposite side of the low mountain area where they'd left their truck.

They found adult teeth, an adult arm and leg bone, and bone fragments that were eventually confirmed to belong to the Jamison family. A further search turned up shoes and bits of clothing. The area in which the bones were found was densely wooded. In this area, there are no paved roads, just dirt ones. This was odd because the Jamison father could not walk more than a few metres without experiencing severe pain, and Sherilynn had chronic pain in her neck and shoulder. Both were on disability, yet they were found on the opposite side of the low mountain area where they'd left their truck.

The hunter who found them said he couldn't work out

why the family had not been found sooner, nor their skeletal remains. He said he was a frequent visitor to the area and so he knew it very well and said that leading up to the spot in which their bodies had lain, there were several trails that would have led anyone searching for them straight to them. He added that one of the skulls had a hole in it. Although the medical examiner later said he couldn't determine if this was a bullet hole or a hole made by an animal, the hunter who found them said he thought the hole was too big to have been made by a bullet. How could the hole have been made?

Both Nikki and Connie say the spot in which their truck was found was a haven for "white supremacists and meth labs and lots of evil people." It was incidentally also where Jessie James once hid out. The new Sheriff is also called Jesse James! If they were shot execution-style, lined up in a row and landing face-down in the dirt, why wasn't their truck searched and their money stolen. The only thing that was missing was the brown brief-case. What was in that case? Said former Sheriff and green beret Beauchamp; "Normally you can go through an investigation and one by one, eliminate certain scenarios.

The husband and wife had left their home taking a gun with them. Their skeletal remains showed they had been lying face-down, in a row. The gun has never been found. Had they been followed and targeted for personal or business reasons? They had a very modern well-equipped home and apparently owned several other properties. Some have questioned how they could have afforded this? Were they into illegal activities? Had they been a bad actor to business associates who would not forgive and forget? Or had they stumble across something and seen something they shouldn't have seen? Had a psychopath stumbled across them, forced them out of their truck and killed them, hunting them down for sport, as they were all found in a face down position. Or was it a 'hit?' Or, was it a predator that we cannot yet define? Why were there no tracks, no footprints?

Sherlyn's mother, Connie Kokotan, told newspapers, "There's no way they just wandered off and got lost.'

Their 'abduction' has echoes of eerily similar unexplained missing person's cases that have been documented over the last couple of centuries; the 'abduction' takes place in a remote wilderness area with dense or difficult terrain, despite Bobby's chronic pain making walking any distance very difficult and Sherilynn too being on disability for chronic shoulder pain, leaving no tracks to follow; neither footprints nor tyre tracks; they left no tracks, no scent.

The 'abductors' one assumes, must have had the ability to not only control and transport these people from their truck through rugged terrain; they also left no other vehicle tracks, nor footprints, nor scent. Colton, Sherilynn's adult son, aged 19, who no longer lived with them, said Bobby was an outdoorsman, "He grew up in the county and I mean proper country; he knew nature and he knew what he was doing out there. No way he would have got them lost like that.' When their skeletal remains were found, the official version was that they must have wandered off into the woods and got lost and died of hypothermia. That didn't explain why cadaver dogs led them to a water tower nearby.

Their bodies were found three miles from their truck, but that was as the crow flies. Bobby suffered chronic pain. "When you're going round and up its near to seven," said Starlet, Sherilynn's mother; "No way they could have made it over that ground. Bobby would get in pain walking around the house let alone covering that kind of ground."

How did they get to the other side of the low mountain, leaving no scent, no vehicle tracks, no footprints, no trace...? How did the die? Why did they die? What really happened out there? Did it have anything to do with a cult and their own spiritual battles/ Is there a perfectly reasonable and rational explanation? Or is there something in the woods there that we have yet to define... "Everything seems possible...." Said Sheriff Beauchamp. Was it a psychopath, a 'hit', or a predator we cannot yet define...?

Chapter Twelve

Two vanished in the woods

'Missing hiker's trail littered with questions,' wrote the Denver Post in 2005. Michelle Vanek, 35, disappeared on September 24th 2005, close to the summit of Mount of the Holy Cross in Colorado. That was where she was last seen. She had slumped down on the ground, exhausted and out of water. Selflessly, she implored her hiking partner to go on without her, to reach the summit they had got so close to. When he returned from the summit, she was gone. It remains now a baffling unsolved mystery as to what became of her.

Her disappearance sparked the largest search in the history of Colorado. The mother of four had seemingly vanished without a trace; although there was a spattering of blood left behind, to add to the strange mystery. Did she get back up, stumble somewhere, and fall into a crevice? Or did she naturally succumb to the elements? Was she killed by a predator? Was that why searchers found a spattering of blood in the snow some distance away from where she had last been seen? Or, asks the Denver Post, did a mysterious squatter, who refused to answer the Sheriff's questions have anything to do with her disappearance?

The search for her lasted a week. She had set out on the climb with hiking partner Eric Sawyer. Only one of them returned. The search was thorough, comprehensive and an exhaustive search. 'But the complete story remains elusive,' said The Denver Post. Tim Cochrane, who headed up the search by Vail Mountain Rescue team, said he believed she had to still be up there. "I just can't tell you where." The missing woman and her hiking partner had been talking for months about attempting to hike to the top of the 14,005-foot Holy Cross Mount. A photo taken before they set off, shows her dressed sensibly in hat, gloves, and carrying ski poles but she had only a small water pack. They set off from Halfmoon trailhead early, at around 6.30 am. It would have been at some point after this that her hiking companion Sawyer would have realized he had left his water purifier and lunch in the car. Investigators would later say that the couple made several mistakes on that journey up to the Mount. In fact, Eagle County Sheriff Deputy Mark Linn said, "Eric made the comment after they got started, that he had a bad feeling about the day."

It was noted that, for some reason, they set out on the Halo route – the hardest route. It was longer and more difficult than the one they could have chosen – the easier North Ridge route. As they progressed, Sawyer noted that his companion was having a hard time flanking him. She was dropping behind by up to 60 feet. By 1.30pm, Michelle had emptied her water flask. With just 400 yards to reach the summit, Michelle said she could make it no further and urged Sawyer to carry on up to the summit without her. Deputy Linn said, "Michelle told him she was tired and could not go on." Sawyer said he offered to go back rather than going on alone without her for the 400 yards to the peak, but he said Michelle insisted he reach it. He had scaled 38 of the 53 'fourteeners' in Colorado and it's no surprise that she urged him to get another 14,000-foot climb under his belt. It's also probably no surprise that he agreed and did go on; after all, he knew she would be there when he got back. Except that she wasn't.

Their biggest mistake was made there, said Howard Paul, president of the Colorado Search and Rescue Board. "She's in a position now where she can't be seen because perhaps she fell, because she started moving, because she couldn't wait any longer, because it was cold. You see this chain link of events – any of which, had they not occurred, the situation would not have happened."

As Sawyer left her to reach the peak, he told her to stay there or begin the downward hike by traversing toward the East Cross Creek trail, and he would catch up with her. "He arrived at the summit at 1.43 pm," said Linn. At the summit, Sawyer phoned his wife to tell her they were running late; they had taken far longer to get to the top than Sawyer had anticipated. Two witnesses spotted him on the summit. They said he was on the summit for roughly 5 minutes. One of the witnesses,

Julia Taylor, spoke with him and he must have told her about his hiking partner because she told the Denver Post; "He just seemed to be in a rush to get back to his partner." She and Sawyer quickly took photos of each other on the summit, for posterity, to show they'd reached it, and then he took off back down to meet up with Michelle.

A short while later, witness Julia Taylor and her husband Bill, who was with her, said they started hearing Sawyer shouting what they thought was "Help!" but in hindsight they realized he could have been shouting "Michelle!" He got no replies.

Over the following week, the biggest search in Colorado history was carried out. More than 700 personnel scoured the area. Helicopters flew overhead. Teams of dogs were brought in to find her scent. Climbers scaled down the ridges of rock formations, and volunteers in huge numbers helped out in the search effort. Every crevice, every drainage area was examined. "We have not seen any tracks and we've not had any responses to our calls and whistles," said Tim Cochrane of the Vail Mountain Rescue Group.

A tempting clue was found when searchers discovered a watch hanging on a tree. This had to be hers they thought; this had to be the route she had taken, and they were now tantalisingly following her trail. Or were they?There were other strange incidents; a hiker coming down the trail refused to talk to searchers, and they came across a tent with a light on inside but the occupant refused to unzip it or respond to their questions. Searcher Brenda Parks said she and her partner ran into a man who refused to talk to them and then hid behind a tree to hide his face. Then he ran down a hill. Neither the searchers nor investigators spoke with him, but the following day, searchers confronted a "suspicious person" in a yellow tent with a light on inside. Sheriff Linn said the person refused to respond to them and would not unzip the tent to speak to them.

Why didn't they simply unzip it?! Later, they saw a man coming off the trail and they believed this was the same person who had been inside the tent. He eventually gave them his name but said he had no id. The day after, investigators believe they met the occupant, but again, he was very reticent to talk with them, refusing to give any i.d. and finally just giving them his name. Having said that, investigators decided they did not think he played any role in the woman's disappearance though. Her hiking companion, Sawyer was ruled out by investigators.

Though he refused to be questioned without a lawyer present, investigators did rule him out as having had nothing at all to do with her disappearance. Without any evidence against him, Sheriff's said, his account could not be disputed. At the time, Michelle's husband Ben said he did not feel her hiking partner had done anything to her either. Though her husband was saddened by Sawyer's decision to leave her alone while he went to the summit, he didn't think foul play had occurred.

As night arrived on the day of her disappearance, a storm blew in, bringing torrents of rain and snow too. Michelle had no tent, no food, no water. Her hiking companion said they hadn't prepared better as they had only planned to be out for the day. Four days later, searchers came across a duffle bag, which contained a shotgun. This was just off Cross Creek Trail. The same day, tracker dogs discovered a few spots of blood in the snow, just south of the Summit. This blood was never determined to be from a person however.

Seven days later, it was reported that 336 searchers, comprising both trained S&R and many volunteers, continued the search, crawling in boulder fields on their hands and knees, inch by inch. They searched the wooded areas below the tree line. They found nothing; her ski poles were not found, she was not found. "It's unprecedented to have 200 searchers on one mountain," said Bill Kaufman, spokesman for the Eagle County Sheriff's Office. "There are nooks and crannies where people could look for shelter. They were literally doing an arm-to-arm, fingertip-to-finger-tip search. There is clue to indicate what directions she went."

Tim Cochrane of the Vail Mountain Rescue Group said five tracker dogs had been taken to the spot where Michell had sat down but they could pick up no scent;

Where had she gone, and her ski poles too? "There's no clue to indicate where she went. We have not seen any tracks," said Cochrane, head of the Vail SAR team, "It's truly a mystery...."

~~~

On June 19, 2015, Cochise County Sheriff's Office in Arizona made the following statement. "Janet Castrejon was last seen outside a campground bathroom in Rustler Park Campground in the Coronado National Forest." This is high in the Chiricahaus Mountains.

NBC News reported, 'Eduado Castrejon says Janet (his daughter) had gone to mail a letter at the pay station not far from where they parked their camper and stopped to use the restroom. Janet was going to wait outside, but when her mother came out of the bathroom, she was gone!"

Her father Eduardo said "My wife ran up to our camping spot to see if she had made it back here, but she never got back. I was here and never saw her. We immediately started searching for her, asking other campers.Their sense of panic and fear for the well-being of their daughter was intensified because although Janet was 44 years old, she had suffered traumatic brain injury in her twenties, which had left her with terrible damage. She was partially blind now and her brain function had been severely impaired, so she was incredibly vulnerable. "Please, for my daughter's sake, if you saw something at all, come forward. We're worried because she can't see and people may not believe her. She was my constant companion. She needs help now!" her father urged reporters.

The family had been on a camping trip. It was Father's Day weekend. They had made plans to spend the weekend in Rustler Park with Oscar, her brother, and several Church members. Rustler Park is a wildflower-carpeted meadow lined by pines and fir trees and set amid a rugged wilderness area high in the Chiricahuas Mountains in Douglas, Arizona. It's a very popular hiking and camping destination.

The family had camped there several times before. This

trip had started out just like the others. The family had left their home in Las Crues on Thursday 18th June and by evening they had arrived in Deming in New Mexico, where they stopped at a Church and then stayed for the night in their camper. The next day after breakfast, they left for Arizona, arriving at the Rustler Park Campground somewhere between 1.30 pm and 2 pm. They were anticipating Janet's elder brother arriving later that evening. At 4 pm they ate a late lunch prepared by her father. After lunch, at approximately 5 pm, her mother Lydia said she wanted to go for a walk and she asked Janet if she wanted to go with her. At first, Janet said she didn't want to go, says her father, but he says; "I said, "Go, honey, so you can take the payment to the pay station." Janet agreed to go.

So, Janet and her mother walked off about 1,000 feet from the camper, according to reports including Las Cruces Sun News, 'down a curved path to the pay station, where Janet deposited the payment envelope.'Her father says, "About 300 feet from the pay station there's a bathroom and my wife decided to go to the bathroom." Janet's mother said Janet didn't need the bathroom, and so she started walking the very short distance back to the camper where her father was. "On her way over, she just disappeared."

After only a couple of minutes, her mother emerged from the bathroom and returned to the camper to find only her husband there. Janet was not there. Her mother said panic began to set in immediately as she and her husband began to search for her in the immediate campground area, shouting her name and whistling but they received no replies and they could not see her.

Her parents said there were no footprints going off the main path. There were no signs of a struggle to suggest their daughter had been attacked and no signs she had suffered an accident. They'd heard no shouts for help, no screams, no cries. "There was nothing there," said her father.

When their son Oscar arrived as planned, three hours later, he called 911. Unfortunately, it was not until another 4 hours had passed that help arrived. The

Cochise County Sheriff's office, along with a Search and Rescue team began hunting for their daughter around half past midnight, according to Carol Capas, spokeswoman for the Sheriff's office. The search lasted all night, until 6 am. No sign of their daughter was found. A fresh search began at 9 am the following morning.

A helicopter was brought in to search overhead. As a new week began, searchers were still trying to find any sign of her or any clues. "We were not able to find Janet," said spokeswoman Capas, adding that the Sheriff's rescue team has continued, on a semi-monthly basis, to canvas the park in search of the missing woman. "This is one of those cases that's unfortunate that it's happened, but it's not like we're going to close it," she said.

Oddly, Las Cruces Sun News reported 'Capas added that a man camping at the park disappeared under similar circumstances not long after Janet was reported missing.' Who was this man? And what happened to him?

Her parents' terror over what might have happened to their daughter, who had vanished within such a tiny distance, in broad daylight, was compounded by the fact that Janet was almost blind. Janet's near-fatal car crash, which occurred just after she'd finished her first semester at New Mexico University, where she'd been studying computer science, had left her with life-changing injuries. She'd been in a coma for 3 months and lost significant amounts of her memory. Her brain function now was limited, and she suffered from short-term memory loss. She was now, as a result, completely dependent on her parents.

Her brother Oscar expressed frustration that disabled people alerts do not exist. He told newspapers, 'If this would have been a child, there immediately would have been an alert – everyone would have known. As each search failed to find any hints or any clues as to where their daughter might be, her other brother Fabian reportedly grew frustrated with the search effort. His father said that Fabian had played a central role in the search effort, spending 3 weeks organising search parties and searching with them, and finding tips and leads for the detectives assigned to the case.

Fabian had felt that enough wasn't being done. Janet's other brother Oscar was also critical. "They assumed too quickly that she was a competent person and they told us that she ran away or left with someone. We specifically told them; she's disabled, she wasn't capable of many, many things..."

After all the intensive searches failed to find any trace of Janet, her family, according to Newspapers, were said to have come to the conclusion that she was lured away. Fabian said, "We believe that somebody took her out or that she got into a car. There's no way she could have strayed too far. That campground is land-locked. The only way to get out of that is the same (way) you come in. There's no real cliff you could fall or, or river to drown in."

This is of course a possibility; the family drove in, so an abductor too could drive in and drive back out, having snatched Janet; and yet, it happened within such a short distance from the family's camper, without shouts or screams or cries. What happened to the other camper too, that the Sherriff's spokeswoman said vanished in the same way, before Janet...?

Chapter Thirteen

The Returned Children

Strange and anomalous cases of odd disappearances and deaths are nothing new. From the days of Charles Fort to John Keel, from antiquity and the Old Testament, to the modern era, cases abound of inexplicably displaced and deceased persons, whose journey to their end makes no sense at all.

A friend kindly sent me some very curious cases from the archives of Newpapers in rural Somerset, West England, from the 1800's. From the Sherborne Mercury of January 9th 1826, for example, comes this odd case; At Chard a man is found in the morning standing against a tree by the river with his throat slit and no memory of the deed or how he came to be in Chard.

'It appears that he had been subject to aberretitions of

the mind and had travelled from Yeovil in the course of the night. He recollected having heard the clock strike 4 as he reached the conduit but nothing subsequently till he found himself in the situation we have described.'

'On further examination it was found his throat was severly cut and the wind pipe nearly severed' The ground around his feet was covered in blood.

And again from the Somerset Mercury of November 14th, 1836; 'An Account of the Melancholy Death of James George, Head Game Keeper at Dunster; Several months before his death, James George went missing for a day and a night.'

'On being questioned as to the cause of his absence, he stated that being on the hill in the park he saw some birds flying far above him which he watched for a time, when he became insensible and continued riding about all night, not knowing where he was'.

From that time, he appeared in a low and melancholy state and suffering from great mental excitement.' He then went missing a few months later on a Tuesday and, 'more than a hundred persons went over the domain in every direction but no trace of him could be discovered'. He was found dead and drowned on the Thursday of that week.

From the Sherborne Mercury of May 30th 1836; 'About six weeks ago, a substantial farmer residing near Chard Someretshire had been transacting business in the neighbouring market town and was remounting his horse in a dreadful state of intoxication, when a friend remonstrated with him for wanting to ride in such a state.'

'He replied that 'He could ride to hell in a quarter of an hour'. Awful to relate, he was found dead on the road having fallen from his horse at a spot just a quarter of an hours ride from town.'

~~~~

And now for our last case; In 1906, three children went into a field and disappeared. The field, called 'forty acres,' was situated a mile outside the town of

Gloucester in the county of Gloucestershire, in the West of England near the Welsh border.

It was recorded by author of the unexplained, Harold T. Wilkins, who was actually one of the many who went out into the fields and woods to search for the missing children. The Vaughan children, a boy aged 10, a girl aged 5, and her sister aged 3, were playing in the field when suddenly they were gone.

"We paid particular attention to the corner of the field where the pasture was bordered by tall old elms and a thick hedge of brambles and a deep ditch separating it from a corn field. Everywhere was probed with sticks and not a stone unturned. Had a dead dog been dumped there, it would certainly have been found."

The strange and inexplicable disappearance of the three young children was reported in the National Newspapers, and concerned readers sent mail orders for money to help with the search, while a reward was put up for any information leading to their whereabouts. When the local vicar called on the children's father, to offer his support and condolences, their father, described as a 'rough and ready' railway brakesman, sent him away, telling him he did not want a visit from a Man of God.

Four frantic days later, after repeated searches of the field, the ditch, the woods adjoining the field and all the area surrounding it, a ploughman starting work in the cornfield at 6am looked over the hedge and saw the three missing children asleep in the ditch.

The children, when asked by everyone what had happened to them, said that they had no idea at all about where they had been or what had happened to them in the 3 days and nights they had been gone.

The ploughman was denied any part of the reward money – on the grounds that he could have kidnapped the children – but this didn't make any sense, as the reward had not been offered when the three children had first disappeared. There was also no evidence to even suggest this was a possibility and the ploughman lived in the tiny village nearby, which was so small that everyone knew everyone else's business intimately.

The male child, when he became an adult, continued to say that he had no idea where they had been or what had happened to them in the 3 days and 3 nights they had been gone.

~~~~

I hope you have enjoyed this book. If you have enjoyed it, perhaps you would be kind enough to leave a review, Thank you so much,

Steph

If you have experienced something strange & unusual, that's hard to explain, please feel free to let me know at

https://www.stephyoungauthor.com/

I'm actively continuing to research and would be very interested.

I also have a Podcast:
Unexplained Mysteries with Steph Young

https://www.patreon.com/stephyoungpodcast

Also by Steph Young:
Panic in the Woods
Stalked in the Woods
Demons: True Stories
True Stories of Real Time Travelers
Haunted Asylums

Creepy Tales of Unexplained Disappearances
Panic in the Woods
Unexplained Disappearances & Mysterious Deaths

Predators in the Woods

Desolating Spirits
An investigation into the 'The Smiley Face Killers.'
Dead in the Water
Encounter with The Unknown

And many more ...

https://www.amazon.com/Steph-Young/e/B00KE8B6B0

Made in the USA
Middletown, DE
04 February 2024

49094629R00146